THE CIVILIZATION OF THE AMERICAN INDIAN SERIES

Pre-Columbian Literatures of Mexico

PRE-COLUMBIAN LITERATURES OF MEXICO

by Miguel León-Portilla

Translated from the Spanish by Grace Lobanov and the Author

UNIVERSITY OF OKLAHOMA PRESS : NORMAN AND LONDON

BY MIGUEL LEÓN-PORTILLA

La Filosofía Náhuatl (Mexico City, 1956, 1959, 1965)

Ritos, Sacerdotes, y Atavíos de los Dioses (Mexico City, 1958)

The Broken Spears: Aztec Account of the Conquest of Mexico (Boston, 1962)

Los Antiguos Mexicanos a Través de sus Crónicas y Cantares (Mexico City, 1961, 1968)

The Broken Spears: Aztec Account of the Conquest of Mexico (Boston, 1962)

Los Antiguos Mexicanos a Través de sus Crónicas y Cantares (Mexico City, 1961, 1968)

Aztec Thought and Culture: A Study of the Ancient Náhuatl Mind (Norman, 1963)

Pre-Columbian Literatures of Mexico (translated by Grace Lobanov and the author) (Norman, 1969)

Native Mesoamerican Spirituality (edited) (Ramsey, N.J., 1980)

LC: 79-32551

ISBN: 0-8061-1974-8

Pre-Columbian Literatures of Mexico is Volume 92 in *The Civilization of the American Indian Series.*

4   5   6   7   8   9   10   11   12   13   14   15   16   17   18   19   20   21

Contents

Illustrations

Preface to the Paperback Edition

Now that this book has been in print in Spanish and English for more than twenty years, I accept the challenge of stating what I deem to be its merit. No doubt, other valuable contributions existed before which presented one or another of the classical texts of these pre-Columbian literatures. But I believe one waited for a concise and also comprehensive and documented introduction to the great corpus of literary productions of Mesoamerica.

My uninterrupted dialogue with people in the academic world and with many other interested persons, mainly in the United States and Mexico, has been particularly rewarding. I have seen that this little book has helped them to discover the rich universe of meaning and beauty which these indigenous productions convey.

The number of students and other people who feel attracted by this literary legacy has increased enormously. At the present time, not only in Mexico and the United States but elsewhere in this hemisphere, in Europe and other more distant countries, such as Israel and Japan, more and more people want to know about and enjoy these ancient classics of the New World.

And there has been another at least equally significant reaction which ought to be mentioned. The indigenous peoples of the New World are becoming much more acquainted with these creations which particularly belong to them. I know Native Americans in Mexico and the United States for whom this ancient world is a radiant source of inspiration.

Now that in many universities and among larger numbers of persons these pre-Columbian literatures are an object of study, research, and enjoyment, one can see also that in several native communities in Mexico the reading of these texts mingles with the recitation of their new poems, chants, and narrations. Indeed, it is true that a new Indian literature is being produced in this hemisphere. The new voices transmit different messages, but if you listen carefully, you will perceive that there is always a hidden link with the past.

I have accepted the challenge to address the possible merit this small book may have. Perhaps it is presumptuous to believe that it has exerted an influence. The only thing I know is that I have seen it in the hands of a good number of colleagues, students, and other people, among them some Native Americans.

Mexico City   MIGUEL LEÓN-PORTILLA

Preface to the First Edition

THE LITERARY PRODUCTIONS of ancient Mexico are now beginning to receive considerable attention. For several decades a humanistic type of research, in an effort to discover and study native codices and other literary texts, has been concerned with the cultures that flourished for thousands of years in this part of the Americas. Archaeology began by unearthing and analyzing the rich material remains, which resulted in establishing more and more accurate chronological sequences and cultural patterns. Later came the aesthetic approach which outlined and began to evaluate the various art forms found in pre-Columbian works. More recently attention has been focused on the codices and texts in order to penetrate into the world of symbols, ideas, and sentiments, which bind together what has justly been called the literary legacy of ancient Mexico.

Linguistics, philology, history, a humanistic awareness, and a critical eye have all played their part in analyzing and studying the manuscripts which contain collections of hymns, poems, and songs and the annals and chronicles, as well as discourses by the elders, legends, and narrative and instructive prose. The work has only begun, but, without any recourse to fantasy, pre-Columbian literary productions can now be presented with considerable accuracy. These are the works left by the wise men and the men living close to the artists who built the great religious centers and who were the early masters of mural painting, sculpture, ceramics, and other arts.

The compositions presented in the following pages are part of the spiritual heritage of the Aztecs, their many neighbors and predecessors who spoke the same Náhuatl language, and also of some groups of the great Maya family. To a lesser extent, there are also examples from the Mixtecs and Zapotecs of Oaxaca, the Tarascans of Michoacán, and the forgotten Otomís of Central Mexico.

However, many questions immediately come to mind. How did these peoples manage not only to conceive but to preserve and transmit their literary legacy? How were they able to save it from destruction during the Conquest and pass it down, at least in part, to the present? A study of the sources, the codices and the ancient texts, will provide the answer and will also open the way to an appreciation of the literary works themselves. I will present a number of examples of the texts, including myths and sacred hymns, lyric poetry, rituals of religious festivals, the beginning of drama, and various forms of prose, accompanied by criticism and brief comments. By way of conclusion attention will be given to the final and most dramatic of the indigenous literary testimonies: the native chronicles of the Conquest, where can be found the point of view of the vanquished.

My intention has not been to write an erudite work on the subject, but to bring to the contemporary reader an understanding of the marvelous world of symbolism which is the very substance of these early literatures. The examples I have chosen from the many which could be cited show the intensely human appeal which these literatures, born in isolation, have for anyone interested in man's adventures with ideas and sentiments.

Originally published in Spanish in 1964, this book has now been re-shaped and somewhat enriched for the English-reading public. In the preparation of this version I have had the good fortune to work closely with the translator, and I have constantly checked the examples quoted against the original texts in the indigenous languages. I dare to say that this English version can be accepted as a faithful translation from the native sources. I wish to express here my thanks to Mrs. Grace Lobanov, who has collaborated with me during an entire year as translator, and to Fernando Horcasitas for reading and criticizing the manuscript.

National University of Mexico   Miguel León-Portilla

Pre-Columbian Literatures of Mexico

Pronunciation Note

The orthography used in this book for words from the various Indian languages of Mexico follows the system introduced by the Spanish missionaries immediately after the Conquest. In general, it can be stated that all of the vowels and most of the consonants have phonetic values very similar to those they have in Spanish. There are, however, some important exceptions:

(1) *h* is pronounced with a soft aspiration as in English.

(2) *tl*, frequent in Náhuatl, the language of the Aztecs, and *ts* and *tz* represent single sounds and therefore should not be divided.

(3) *u* before *a, e, i,* and *o* is pronounced like the English *w*.

(4) *x*, as in sixteenth-century Spanish, has the same sound as the English *sh*.

(5) The Maya languages are rich in glottalized consonants to be pronounced with a constricted throat.

(6) Practically all Náhuatl words are accented on the next to last syllable. Many Maya words, on the other hand, have the stress on the last syllable. Accent is often indicated today by accent marks used according to rules of Spanish accentuation.

Background and Sources

THERE IS PROBABLY no more eloquent picture of the inner and outer life of any culture than its literary production. In the case of ancient cultures, if a literary legacy remains, it serves as key to a deeper understanding of the past. There would be very little known about the Near East, the Far East, Greece, and Rome without their literatures. In the broadest sense literature includes oral tradition, inscriptions, and the contents of codices, texts, and documents. These contain the myths and legends, the chronicles and history, ritual hymns, a variety of poetry, discourses, the beginnings of the theater, and governmental and religious proclamations —in other words, an image of the everyday life of a people.

In the case of ancient Mexico, where isolated cultures flourished for thousands of years, it is stimulating to study their arts as uncovered by archaeology. But it is equally fascinating to delve into their ways of thinking, feeling, and acting as expressed in their literary creations. Some inscriptions in stone have been deciphered, there are documents and manuscripts in archives and libraries, and there are a few pre-Columbian codices or painted books. The origin of the documents and other evidence of the oldest literary works in the Americas and the ways in which they were transmitted and preserved will be discussed at some length. Special consideration will be given to the creative works remaining from some groups of the Maya family, from those who spoke Náhuatl, the language of the Aztecs, and from other groups such as the Mixtecs and Zapotecs of Oaxaca, the Tarascans of Michoacán, and the Otomís of Central Mexico.

A brief survey of the evolution of these peoples will further under-

3

standing of their literary expressions. Starting from the more familiar historical moment when the Spanish conquerors arrived in 1519, the survey will proceed backward through the years to uncover the roots of pre-Columbian civilization in Mexico.

The Aztecs at the Beginning of the Sixteenth Century

When the Spaniards arrived in Central Mexico in November, 1519, they were amazed at the splendor of the Aztec metropolis, Mexico-Tenochtitlan. Hernán Cortés in his letters to Charles V, Bernal Díaz del Castillo in his history, and the other Spanish chroniclers of the Conquest described the beauty and magnificence of the palaces and temples, the great plaza with its seventy-eight ceremonial buildings, the market, the gardens and orchards, and the streets, canals, and causeways which linked the island with the mainland.

But it was not only the pyramids, sculpture, and painting which astonished the conquerors. They came to know something about the organization of the political, social, and religious life of the Aztecs. They saw the power and wealth of Moctezuma, the shrewdness of the merchants, the endurance of the warriors and their captains, and the subtlety and wisdom of the priests and leaders who not only presided over religious affairs but also advised the supreme ruler. The priests were in charge of educating the young people; they were custodians of esoteric knowledge, wisdom, and tradition, of the two calendars, and of the art of writing in painted books and inscriptions. Bernal Díaz del Castillo, the soldier and chronicler, described the houses and the schools and temples where priests and wise men guarded "the many books of paper folded like Castilian clothes."[1]

A few years later the first Franciscan missionaries were even more impressed to discover the historical records, the myths, and the traditions of the people. It is not necessary to repeat here what happened to most of those books as a consequence of the religious zeal of the friars. But while many missionaries were collecting manuscripts for the pyre, Bernardino de Sahagún and a few others managed to save some of the old texts in order to study the native past.

[1] *Historia verdadera de la Conquista de la Nueva España*, I, 143.

4

The painted books, folded sheets of paper made from bark of the *amate* tree or wild fig (*ficus petiolaris*) or from treated deerskin coated with a white pigment, were used by the Aztec wise men to preserve their knowledge and also to educate the youth. In Mexico-Tenochtitlan and throughout the country there were many kinds of schools, but the best known were the *telpochcalli* or houses for young people and the *calmécac* or centers of higher learning. In both these schools, but principally in the *calmécac*, the painted books containing the myths, historical events, and even some religious doctrines expressed in ideograms were studied and explained. The old hymns, poems, and chronicles were learned by heart. Sahagún described the method of instruction used by the native wise men: "They taught them to sing all the verses of the songs which are called divine. The verses were written in their books with characters. . . . They also taught them Indian astrology, the meaning of dreams and the count of the years."[2] Thus the Aztecs preserved and transmitted their literary and religious legacy by memorizing the texts of their ancient wisdom as recorded in the codices by means of pictograms and ideograms.

But who invented this system of education and the writing of codices? Actually, the Aztecs arrived in the valley of Mexico in the middle of the thirteenth century A.D. and, after much suffering and persecution, succeeded in establishing their capital on an island in the middle of the lake in 1325. They became independent only in 1428 after defeating the former rulers, the Tecpanecs of Azcapotzalco. Then, almost incredibly, in less than a century they won hegemony over the central and southern portions of what is today the Republic of Mexico. The Aztec splendor which preceded the Spanish Conquest was historically brief.

The origin of writing and the system of education in ancient Mexico can be traced in archaeology and native sources. The Aztecs, like the Tezcocans, the people of Tlaxcala, and many other groups speaking the Náhuatl language, were actually a strain of a much older culture. Many of the religious ideas, the social and political organizations, the calendars, writing, and many techniques of the arts were received either directly or

---

[2] *Historia General de las Cosas de Nueva España*, I, 307. All references are to the A. M. Garibay K. edition.

indirectly by acculturation, through contact with more advanced peoples. This happened with the Aztecs during their sojourn in the thirteenth and beginning of the fourteenth centuries in territories belonging to the Tecpanecs of Azcapotzalco and the more advanced Culhuacans, who in their turn had inherited much of the earlier Toltec culture.

The Toltecs and the Postclassic Culture

The Toltec metropolis of Tula, some ninety miles north of modern Mexico City, was at its height from the ninth to the eleventh centuries A.D., according to archaeological findings and old Indian chronicles. The Toltecs, as well as the Mixtecs of Oaxaca and the Mayas of northern Yucatán, already knew the art of writing as proved by extant glyphs, stone inscriptions, and some painted books, all of which reveal their high culture. Archaeology accepts the ninth century A.D. as the beginning of the Post-Classic Period of these cultures in ancient Mexico.

The Aztecs often repeated in their texts that the Toltecs were followers of the great wise man and priest, Quetzalcóatl, who taught them many of their arts and their most important religious doctrines. According to the legend, as a consequence of internal conflict and pressure from without, Tula was abandoned around the end of the eleventh century, and groups of migrating Toltecs carried their knowledge and arts with them. Some moved as far as Yucatán. Others remained nearby and mixed with peoples already living in the central plateau, such as the Culhuacans established along the southeastern shore of the lake in the valley of Mexico. The Culhuacans became the principal transmitters of Toltec culture to groups of late-comers from the north, such as the Aztecs.

The Mixtecs of Oaxaca, who have left the largest number of pre-Columbian codices, had a recognizable influence on the people of Central Mexico. The Mixtec art of writing and painting books was very similar to the one used later by the Aztecs and their neighbors, including the Tezcocans. According to Indian sources, wise men from the Mixtec area settled among the Tezcocans, who learned from them various arts including writing.[3] These wise men were called *tlailotlaque*, a word which

---

[3] See Fernando de Alva Ixtlilxóchitl, *Obras Históricas*, I, 117.

means "those-who-came-back," probably referring to the Toltecs who had joined the Mixtecs when Tula was abandoned.

There is also in Central Mexico a hint of possible Maya influence in the bas reliefs of the pyramid at Xochicalco, not far from the modern town of Cuernavaca, where some carved figures related to calendric calculations appear Maya. Although Maya presence is uncertain, it can be stated positively that some ancient Toltec and Mixtec cultural institutions were transmitted to the peoples living during Aztec days in the central highlands of Mexico.

The Toltec, Mixtec, and Maya inscriptions in stone, as well as the representations of priests and wise men speaking and instructing during the Post-Classic Period between the ninth and eleventh centuries A.D., testify to the ancient concern for remembering history. But was it the Toltecs, Mixtecs, and Mayas of this period who invented the calendar, writing, and other systems of preserving knowledge of the past? The answer is found in what archaeologists call the Classic Period of splendor in Mesoamerica.[4]

The Classic Period—First to Eighth Centuries A.D.

In Central Mexico, not very far from the Toltec metropolis of Tula, there is the City of the Gods, built centuries earlier by the Teotihuacans.

In Oaxaca, close to the area where the Mixtecs reached their height, stands Monte Albán, the principal remains of another nation with a much older culture, the Zapotecs; their descendants continue using the ancient language even today.

Finally, older Maya groups living not only in Yucatán but also in the jungles of a large part of Central America had built remarkable ceremonial centers in Copán, Tikal, Uaxactún, Yaxchilán, Palenque, and

---

[4] The term Mesoamerica covers what is today Central and Southern Mexico, plus those areas of Central America where the Mayas and other groups with similar cultural patterns lived in pre-Columbian times. According to the definition adopted by many anthropologists, it designates the area extending across the continent south and eastward from the Sinaloa, Lerma, and Pánuco rivers in Mexico to what is today northwestern Honduras and along the highlands and Pacific Coast of Central America as far as the Nicoya Peninsula of Costa Rica. For a detailed description of the geography of this pre-Columbian cultural area, see Robert Wauchope (ed.), *Handbook of Middle American Indians*, I.

other sites. Archaeologists have discovered temples and palaces erected by pre-Columbian architects which in some cases suggest urban living. There is abundant proof of the existence of various forms of the calendar, writing, and a definite historical consciousness. This classic people left countless inscriptions in their steles, in temples, palaces, and even in ceramics. Most of the Maya hieroglyphs have not been deciphered, but those dealing with the calendar and with certain deities show a long cultural sequence beginning in the early days of the Classic Period and ending with later inscriptions in the three extant Maya codices.

Also, in the case of the Teotihuacans and Zapotecs, some inscriptions and dates have been found. As Alfonso Caso has shown clearly, the Teotihuacans already had the ritual and astrological calendar called *Tonalpohualli* by the Aztecs, *Tzolkin* by the Mayas, and *Piye* by the Zapotecs.[5] The builders of the City of the Gods used the same glyphs which appear later in Aztec codices to represent flower-and-song, an expression which means poetry, water-and-fire which signifies war, and also the ideas of movement and travel, certain attributes of the gods, and other concepts. It must also be noted that the Zapotecs of the Classic Period possessed an older form of writing as shown on stele inscriptions dating before Christ found at their great center of Monte Albán. Later forms of Zapotec writing and the calendar seem to be derived from this older form.

Archaeology has now established a long sequence in the transmission of writing and the calendar, from the Classic Period of Mesoamerica, which shows a common preoccupation shared by different peoples to preserve the memory of their past. The study of architecture, sculpture, painting, ceramics, and the ancient world view as found in the inscriptions, codices, and extant texts of these peoples leads to the assumption that, aside from local differences, these peoples shared a single cultural origin, which is probably the ultimate source of literary creations in later pre-Columbian Mexico.

The question of origins is always extremely difficult. In this case

---

[5] See Alfonso Caso, "¿Tenían los teotihuacanos conocimiento del Tonalpohualli?" *El México Antiguo*, Vol. IV, 131–43, and César Lizardi Ramos, "¿Conocían el Xíhuitl los teotihuacanos?" *El México Antiguo*, Vol. VIII, 220–23.

archaeology has not yet found the answer. But there is considerable evidence which permits a few words about the possible mother culture from which so many peoples derived, among other things, the precious knowledge of writing and the measurement of time.

The Olmecs

Along the coast of the Gulf of Mexico, in the modern Mexican states of Veracruz and Tabasco, a region known to the Aztecs as Rubberland, was the home of the Olmecs. These people dated back more than nine hundred years before Christ. Having identified certain characteristic traits in many of their works, archaeologists have found traces of their presence or at least influence in many other areas, some far away from Rubberland. The oldest inscriptions discovered in Mexico up to now all show some relation to the Olmecs. Among these are the "C" stele found in Tres Zapotes, Veracruz, the inscriptions on the famous Tuxtla jade figurine, and the still more ancient glyphs on the steles at the ceremonial center of Monte Albán in Oaxaca which, as already mentioned, antedate the splendor of Zapotec culture. These Olmec-type inscriptions all point to an invention of the art of recording the past. Alfonso Caso sums up concisely what is known to date about the origins of writing and the calendar in ancient Mexico as a result of archaeological findings:

> According to the Carbon 14 test, it has been determined that there was writing and a calendar system in Mesoamerica at least as early as 600 B.C. But since the calendar of that time shows an extraordinary perfection and is already related to many other aspects of Mesoamerican culture (ceramics, sculpture in stone, jade, pyramids, palaces, and so forth), it can be stated positively that it was the result of a long process of development which began many centuries before the Christian era.[6]

Apparently the same Aztec elders who rescued many texts and poems also knew of the antiquity of the invention of writing and the calendar. In a text in which they speak of the origin of their culture, they say that "in a time which nobody can reckon and about which nobody exactly

---

[6] *"Relaciones entre el Viejo y el Nuevo Mundo. Una Observación Metodológica,"* *Cuadernos Americanos,* Vol. CXXV, 167–68.

remembers," many years before the building of Teotihuacan, along the shores of the Gulf of Mexico lived a people whose wise men and priests possessed many painted books and a knowledge of measuring time. These people appeared in the north, not far from the mouth of the Pánuco River, and among them were

Those who
carried with them
the black and red ink,
the manuscripts and painted books,
the wisdom.
They brought everything with them,
the annals,
the books of song, and their flutes.[7]

These wise men cannot be positively identified as the Olmecs, to whom archaeology has ascribed the oldest writing. However, archaeological discoveries give some support to the Aztec belief that before the days of Teotihuacan there was a people along the Gulf Coast who possessed the art of writing and the calendar. The accepted fact is that the methods of preserving knowledge and memories of the past among the native groups of Mexico have been carried in a cultural sequence with roots over two thousand years old.

This rapid survey of Mexico's past shows that the various nations speaking the Aztec or Náhuatl language, the Mayas, and the peoples of Oaxaca, as well as other groups, were cultural descendants of a people who created a historical consciousness and highly developed institutions. They were totally isolated from the ancient civilizations of Europe and Asia, in possession of their own culture hundreds of years before contact with the Western world resulted in their destruction.

When the Spanish conquerors first came in contact with the Aztecs and Mayas, these peoples still retained much of their ancient cultural heritage. To understand how they managed to preserve the memory of their past and continued to create art and literature, it is necessary to analyze in greater detail their methods of writing and the oral tradition as it was taught in the pre-Columbian centers of education.

[7] *Códice Matritense de la Real Academia*, VIII, fol. 192 r.

The Writing of Codices and Memorizing of Texts

Some native chroniclers and the friars who wrote about the ancient cultures described the oral teaching and the memorizing of texts in pre-Hispanic schools as an indispensable complement to the preservation of the history and doctrines contained in the codices or painted books. For instance, Fray Diego de Durán said that Náhuatl teachers had "large books with beautiful paintings and symbols about all the arts, from which they taught."[8]

Since the wise men realized it was impossible for most people in the community to have their own books and paintings and were also conscious of the limitations inherent in their systems of writing, they insisted on systematic memorizing as a means of preserving tradition and knowledge. Teachers required their students to learn by heart songs, poems, and discourses in which the painted books were explained. When they had memorized the commentary on the codices and learned the doctrine, they too could say with the Náhuatl poet,

I sing the pictures of the book
and see them spread out;
I am an elegant bird
for I make the codices speak
within the house of pictures.[9]

The codices or painted books were always the basis of teaching. As one native text says, "Your songs are written, but you spread them out beside the kettle drums." By using their books, native teachers were able to pass on much information without error; they could fix the exact day and year of any happening; they could symbolize abstract concepts of religious belief and relate myths and doctrines. In other words, they could outline schematically the fundamentals of their knowledge and history.

The Aztecs, Tezcocans, and Tlaxcalans, in the days immediately pre-

---

[8] *Historia de las Indias de Nueva España y Islas de Tierra firme*, II, 229.

[9] Antonio Peñafiel (ed.), *Colección de Cantares Mexicanos*, fol. 14 v. The original manuscript is found in the National Library of Mexico.

ceding the Conquest, used three principal kinds of writing: pictograms, ideograms, and a partially phonetic form of inscript.

Pictograms, schematic representation of things, are the most elemental. For example, several Aztec codices show the migration of the seven Náhuatl tribes from the north, schematically represented by figures of *teomamas* or priests carrying the patron gods on their shoulders. There are also the outlines of the *calli* or houses of the *tlachtli* (ball games), the *tlatoque* (lords) seated on their *icpalli* (royal chairs), and of the tributes which included mantles, plumage, cocoa, bundles of corn, and other products.

However, as in other ancient cultures, the Náhuatl scribes advanced from the purely pictographic stage to ideograms or the symbolic representation of ideas. These ideograms were concerned with numerical calculations, the calendar, and other abstract ideas such as movement (*ollin*), life (*yoliliztli*), and divinity (*teotl*). The colors also were symbolic. In the human figure yellow almost always meant the female sex, violet suggested royalty of the *tlatoani* or principal lord, blue represented the south, and red and black meant writing and wisdom.

The understanding and interpretation of ideograms require a long and patient study. It is sufficient to point out that among Náhuatl-speaking peoples, as well as for the Mayas, Mixtecs, and Zapotecs, ideograms were especially important in relation to numbers and to their extremely precise calendars.[10]

In addition to pictographs and ideograms in ancient Mexican writing, there were representations of sounds or the beginnings of phonetic writing. Náhuatl phonetic writing, as found in some of the codices, was used principally for names of people and places. The native scribes developed a system of syllabic inscriptions to represent, among other things, names of persons and places. For instance, by painting a stylized "tooth" (*tlan-tli* in Náhuatl), together with the well-known glyph for "reed" (*ácatl*), they meant to represent phonetically *aca-tlan*, "place of reeds." Finally they succeeded in symbolizing some single letter sounds

[10] For more detail, see Charles E. Dibble, "*El Antiguo Sistema de Escritura en México,*" *Revista Mexicana de Estudios Antropológicos,* Vol. IV, 105–28, and Miguel León-Portilla, *Los Antiguos Mexicanos,* 48–75.

such as "a," "e," and "o," represented by stylized pictographs for *a-tl* (water), *e-tl* (beans), and *o-tli* (road).

The ancient Mexicans made use of these forms of writing to draw codices in which, as Fray Diego de Durán said, "they recorded their memorable deeds, their wars and victories. . . . Everything was written down . . . with hieroglyphics for the year, month, and day when the event happened."[11] In comparing the cultural development of these peoples with that of other civilizations on the basis of their writing, the North American anthropologist Alfred Kroeber wrote: "If one thinks of the invention of the first idea of part-phonetic writing, it is conceivable that all the ancient systems of the Old World derive from a single such invention; although even in that event the Maya-Aztec system would remain as a wholly separate growth."[12]

While these forms of pre-Hispanic Náhuatl writing were being developed on the basis of the ancient Toltec and Teotihuacan inheritance, the peoples of the Maya family had their own systems, more highly developed than those of the central region of Mexico. A great number of inscriptions are preserved from the Maya Classic and Post-Classic periods on stone steles, on staircases and lintels, in the interior of some temples and palaces, and even on ceramics. The Maya codices known as the *Dresden*, the *Paris*, and the *Tro-Cortesiano* which is in Madrid are of a later period but also antedate the Conquest. Up to the present time the numerical and calendric symbols have been deciphered, as well as a few other ideograms concerning the gods and their attributes. The Mayas discovered and represented the concept of the zero and the value of minus numbers before any other culture. Their calendar was one ten-thousandth closer to the tropical year than our Gregorian calendar. They were remarkable masters in the art of recording time.

Unfortunately, in spite of considerable research, many Maya glyphs still remain undeciphered. They are thought to be largely ideographic, possibly containing some phonetic elements. If the inscriptions on the steles, the temples, and palaces can be entirely deciphered, this will undoubtedly give the key to many other texts of literary value.

[11] *Op. cit.*, II, 257.
[12] *Anthropology*, 268.

Also among the Mayas, as among the peoples of Central Mexico, there were schools in which the ancient wisdom and knowledge contained in the painted books were passed on and preserved by memorizing. Fray Diego de Landa said: "These peoples also used characters or symbols to write in their books about their sciences and ancient things; they understood them by means of these figures and signs, and they taught them."[13] As a result of this method of teaching, important literary works have survived from various Maya groups. Some wise men who lived through the Conquest and remembered the pre-Hispanic teachings wrote down many texts in the alphabet brought by the conquerors, but in their own native language and based on the ancient codices which they had been able to save. Researchers began to study and translate these works only around the middle of the nineteenth century.

It is true that the Conquest resulted in the destruction of most of the ancient indigenous codices. However, humanist friars such as Andrés de Olmos and especially Bernardino de Sahagún attempted to rescue as much as possible of the cultural heritage of the pre-Hispanic peoples. As Sahagún came to know their literary legacy, he compared it with that of Greece and Rome: "The same thing happened in this Indian nation, especially among the Mexicans, whose learned, valiant, and virtuous wise men were highly esteemed."[14]

The Sources

The first attempt to preserve native literary texts in the central region of Mexico dates from between 1524 and 1530. During these years Náhuatl wise men, who had probably learned the Latin alphabet from the first twelve friars who came to New Spain, set down in their own language, but in Latin script, the explanations and commentaries of various codices and historical records. Their writings on native paper are preserved today in the National Library of Paris and are known as *Anales de Tlatelolco* or *Anales Históricos de la Nación Mexicana.* There is recorded the gene-

---

[13] *Relación de las Cosas de Yucatán*, 207. All references are to the Héctor Pérez Martínez edition.

[14] *Op. cit.*, II, 53.

alogy of the rulers of Tlatelolco, Mexico-Tenochtitlan, and Azcapotzalco, and also the oldest-known Indian account of the Spanish Conquest.[15]

Fray Andrés de Olmos, who arrived in New Spain in 1528, also set about collecting the greatest possible number of orations and discourses delivered in Náhuatl by wise men and elders before the Conquest. These texts, known as *huehuetlatolli*, are speeches made on important occasions such as the death of a king, the election of a new governor, the birth of a child, or a marriage, as well as the advice given by fathers and mothers to their children and even lectures on morals delivered by teachers. These texts, written from oral accounts by elders who had memorized and recited them before the Conquest, are of considerable value in studying Náhuatl thought. They are now preserved in the Library of Congress in Washington and in the national libraries of Mexico and Paris.[16]

But even more important than the work done by Olmos was the major research undertaken by Fray Bernardino de Sahagún. Some years after his arrival in Mexico in 1529, he prepared a questionnaire covering subjects on which he needed information for a more complete understanding of the indigenous way of thinking. Among other things he was anxious to know more about were the old hymns to the gods and the profane songs, ancient discourses, proverbs and native sayings, the religious doctrines, myths and legends, the calendars, manners and habits of the lords, duties of the priests and wise men, and descriptions of the different occupations such as the artists, merchants, and other people of the community. As Sahagún himself said, he wanted to know about "all the divine or rather idolatrous things, as well as the human and natural things in this New Spain."[17]

With the help of his native students at the Imperial College of Santa Cruz de Tlatelolco, Sahagún began by collecting hundreds of texts from

[15] Vol. II in Ernst Mengin (ed.), *Corpus Codicum Americanorum Medii Aevi.* An English translation of the Indian account of the Conquest included in this document has been published in León-Portilla, *The Broken Spears.*

[16] In Andrés de Olmos, *Arte para aprender la lengua mexicana.* The editor, Remi Simeon, included some of the *huehuetlatolli* collected by this Franciscan missionary. See also Garibay K. (tr.), "*Huehuetlatolli, Documento A.*" *Tlalocan,* Vol. I, No. 1 (1943), 31–53, 81–107.

[17] *Op. cit.,* I, 28.

different parts of Central Mexico. He described the manner in which he began his work: "Everything we discussed was told me by indigenous elders, using pictures, which were their writing in the olden days."[18] While the older Indians recalled the ancient doctrines and texts, the young Tlatelolcan students wrote down everything in their own language, but in Latin script. They also copied as many as possible of the figures and ideograms from the codices which the elders treasured. With a critical eye, Sahagún repeated his questions several times, "putting the material through a sieve three times," as he expressed it, to be certain of its authenticity.

This well-planned and lengthy research, to which Sahagún devoted the greater part of the sixty years he lived in New Spain, yielded an enormous collection of almost one thousand folios written on both sides, with pictures and the text in Náhuatl. This material, which passed through many vicissitudes, served Sahagún as the basis for his *Historia General de las Cosas de Nueva España,* which is not an exact translation of the Náhuatl texts but rather a summarized presentation of the main subjects with comments.[19] The documents written down in Náhuatl for Sahagún went to Spain by order of Philip II. There is a copy of them in the Laurentian Library in Florence, catalogued as the *Florentine Codex.*[20] The original manuscripts, known as *Códices Matritenses,* are still preserved in the Royal Palace and in the Library of the Academy of History in the Spanish capital.[21]

Sahagún's work had further consequences. Some of his students, awakened to an interest in the preservation of their ancient culture, continued of their own accord the task of transcription. Antonio Valeriano of Azcapotzalco, Martín Jacobita and Andrés Leonardo of Tlatelolco,

---

[18] *Ibid.,* I, 106.

[19] See the introduction to León-Portilla, *Ritos, Sacerdotes y Atavíos de los Dioses,* 9–37.

[20] For a Náhuatl-English edition, see Arthur J. O. Anderson and Charles E. Dibble (trs. and eds.), *Florentine Codex,* which contains the Náhuatl text corresponding to Books I–V and VII–XII of Sahagún's *Historia General.*

[21] Between 1905 and 1907 the Mexican scholar Francisco del Paso y Troncoso prepared a facsimile edition of all the material contained in the *Códices Matritenses.* A list of bilingual editions taken from the original texts in Náhuatl, which have been published to date, is found in the bibliography at the end of this book.

and Alonso Begerano and Pedro de San Buenaventure of Cuauhtitlán all recorded in the indigenous language various collections of pre-Hispanic songs and an entire set of historical documents. Among the latter are the *Anales de Cuauhtitlán* and the *Legend of the Suns*.[22]

In these manuscripts are found myths about the cosmological ages or suns, a version of the legend of Quetzalcóatl, and historical records belonging to the principal towns in the central part of Mexico. These native students and others like Juan de Pomar are responsible for the compilation and transcription of three important texts in poetry: the *Colección de Cantares Mexicanos* which is now in the National Library of Mexico, the so-called *Manuscrito de los romances de los señores de la Nueva España* in the Latin American Collection of the University of Texas, and another collection of songs preserved at the National Library of Paris.[23] In these three are several hundred poems, mostly of pre-Hispanic origin, some by such famous poets as Nezahualcóyotl of Tezcoco and Tecayehuatzin of Huexotzinco. Also important is the *Libro de los coloquios*, which includes the discussions which took place in the courtyard of the San Francisco monastery in Mexico City in 1524 between the first monks who came to New Spain and Náhuatl elders and priests who defended their way of thinking and their beliefs.[24] All these texts are important, but the collections of songs and poems in Náhuatl are of special interest. Most of the epic and lyric writings, the love poems, and also the dramatic verse which will be presented here are from these collections.

There are other indigenous documents such as the *Historia Tolteca-Chichimeca* in the National Library of Paris and the *Aubin Codex* written

[22] *Anales de Cuauhtitlán* and *Leyenda de los Soles* are in the *Códice Chimalpopoca*. Walter Lehmann has published the paleography and the German translation of the text in *Die Geschichte der Königreiche von Colhuacan und Mexico.*

[23] The paleography and the Spanish version of these manuscripts have been prepared by A. M. Garibay K., *Poesía Náhuatl*, I–II.

[24] *Colloquios y Doctrina Christiana con que los Doze Frayles de San Francisco enviados por el Papa Adriano Sesto y por el Emperador Carlos Quinto convertieron a los Indios de la Nueva Espanya en Lengua Mexicana y Española.* The text was discovered in the Secret Archives of the Vatican in 1924 by Father Pascual Saura. Walter Lehmann has published the paleography of the text with a German version in *Sterbende Götter und Christliche Heilbotschaft.*

with ancient ideograms and partly annotated in Náhuatl in Latin script.[25] It is obviously impossible to mention here all the manuscripts, some of which are not entirely literary in nature. Angel María Garibay K. lists them in his *Historia de la Literatura Náhuatl.*[26]

It only remains to mention that at the end of the sixteenth and beginning of the seventeenth centuries several natives and mestizos, including Don Fernando Alvarado Tezozómoc, Chimalpain, and Ixtlilxóchitl, who were conversant with the European manner of writing history, worked out in detail their own accounts in Náhuatl or Spanish based principally on pre-Hispanic documents. In their effort to defend their traditions and ancient way of life to the Spanish world, they preserved many texts which are obviously pre-Columbian.[27]

These are the principal sources of Náhuatl indigenous literature which have come down to the present. Other pre-Columbian texts come from the various groups of Maya culture.

Among the Mayas of Yucatán and the Quichés and Cakchiquels of Guatemala there were also wise men, usually descended from priests or nobles, who after the Conquest began to transcribe the traditions taught in pre-Hispanic schools and the content of ancient codices, especially those concerned with history and the calendar. This effort to preserve ancient knowledge has compensated somewhat for the loss of the Maya codices; as already mentioned, only three of these remain and they are largely undeciphered.

This work of the elders preserved various chronicles, some books on native medicine, and a whole series of texts known under the general title of *Chilam Balam*, written in the Maya language of Yucatán in Latin script.[28]

Probably the most ancient Maya manuscript is that known as *Crónica de Chicxulub* [*Chac-Xulub-Chen*], the name of the town where it was

[25] Facsimile edition of *Historia Tolteca-Chichimeca* is Vol. I in Ernst Mengin (ed.), *Corpus Codicum Americanorum Medii Aevi.*

[26] I, 51–56.

[27] See León-Portilla, *Aztec Thought and Culture*, 195–97.

[28] See Alfredo Barrera Vásquez and Sylvanus G. Morley, *The Maya Chronicles*, 1–86.

written in the middle of the sixteenth century by an Indian noble, Nakuk Pech. Although only twenty-six pages long, it is of great interest because it contains, among other things, a Maya account of the Spanish Conquest.

Among the writings on indigenous medicine, most of which are of a later date, are the *Libro de Medicina*, the *Cuaderno de Teabo*, the *Noticias de varias plantas*, the *Libro de los Médicos*, and the *Ritual de los Bacaab*, all by unknown authors and only partially studied.[29]

The books of *Chilam Balam* are without doubt the most significant part of what remains of early Maya literature. The *chilames*, or more exactly *chilamoob*, were from the upper echelon in the priestly hierarchy of pre-Hispanic times. They served as teachers and sometimes acted as prophets. The Maya specialist Alfredo Barrera Vásquez recalls that *Balam* is "the name of the most famous of the *chilames* who lived a little before the arrival of the white men. *Balam* is a family name which means jaguar or witch, in a figurative sense."[30]

There are eighteen known *Chilam Balam* books still in existence. Up to now four have been partly studied and translated. These contain prophecies of the days, the years, and longer periods of time. There are also mythical and historical passages, hymns and songs, and tradition and ancient wisdom interspersed with ideas obviously Christian and biblical in origin. The best known of these texts is the *Chilam Balam of Chumayel*, of which only a late version exists, copied at the end of the eighteenth century. According to Antonio Mediz Bolio, this manuscript has sixteen sections or books. The titles give a glimpse of the variety of subject matter: "Book of Lineage," "The Conquest," "Katún or Twenty Year Period," "The Trials," "The Ancient Gods," "The Spirits," "The Thirteenth Ahau Katún," "Beginnings of the Itzaes," "The Month Book," "Katún of the Flower," "Book of the Mysteries," "Wheel of the Katúns," "List of the Katúns," "Chronicle of the Dzules," "Forecast of the Thirteen Katúns," and "Book of Prophecies." Merely the study of

[29] For a description of these manuscripts, see Alfred M. Tozzer, *A Maya Grammar with Bibliography and Appraisement of the Works Noted*; and Ralph L. Roys (ed.), *Ritual of the Bacabs*.

[30] *El Libro de los Libros de Chilam Balam.*

Chilam Balam of Chumayel would be sufficient to give an idea of the richness of Maya literature and a world of symbolism that could be opened up by more extensive research.[31]

Another of the important *Chilam Balam* books, the one from Tizimín, contains twenty-six pages of mythology, prophecies, and legends. There is an English translation of the Tizimín text prepared by Maud W. Makemson.[32] *The Chilam Balam of Maní*, a part of the *Ixil* book, and the *Crónica de Oxkutzcab* are all found in the *Códice Pérez*, named in honor of Don Juan Pío Pérez who gathered and translated this material into Spanish.

Actually the content of all these Maya texts is similar, including chronicles, prophecies of different *katúns* or twenty-year periods, and some poems and songs. In spite of the elements obviously added from Christianity and the Bible, this material gives a good picture of the historical and literary tradition of the Mayas.[33]

Another work known as *Códice de Calkiní*, sometimes also called *Chilam Balam de Calkiní*, has been published by Barrera Vásquez in a facsimile edition. It is an ancient manuscript about the Mayas who inhabited Calkiní in the modern state of Campeche, and tells of their resistance to the Spanish Conquest. Barrera Vásquez has also recently published a collection of songs, *El libro de los Cantares de Dzitbalché*, containing fifteen poems, some with real dramatic significance.[34] A number of these songs, vigorous examples of Maya poetry, will be discussed in the following pages.

In addition to the texts from Yucatán, there is also a chronicle written in the Maya Chontal language of Tabasco which tells of Hernán Cortés, with Cuauhtémoc as prisoner, arriving in the Acalan region on the coast

[31] See Antonio Mediz Bolio (ed.), *El Libro de Chilam de Chumayel*. Paleography of the Maya text and a more accurate translation is found in Ralph L. Roys (ed.), *The Book of Chilam Balam of Chumayel*.

[32] *The Book of the Jaguar Priest*, 14.

[33] An annotated list of all the different books of *Chilam Balam* can be found in Barrera Vásquez and Morley, *op. cit.*

[34] This work gives the paleography of the Maya manuscript and a translation into Spanish.

of the Gulf of Mexico. The principal interest of this text is Cuauhtémoc's bid for Chontal support against the Spanish conquerors.[35]

The Quiché and Cakchiquel peoples, branches of the Maya family in Guatemala, have also left a rich literary legacy. The most important manuscripts in the Quiché tongue are the famous *Popol Vuh* or "Book of the People," the *Títulos de los Señores de Totonicapán*, and the *Rabinal Achí*, a pre-Hispanic play.

The *Popol Vuh* is probably the most widely known native American text. Although written after the Conquest and containing obvious interpolations of Christian origin, it preserves pre-Columbian tradition and history. It was not until the beginning of the eighteenth century that Fray Francisco Ximénez, parish priest of Chichicastenango in Guatemala, happened to discover the old manuscript. Already interested in Indian antiquities, Father Ximénez immediately copied the text, which was in the Quiché tongue, and made a translation into Spanish entitled *Historias del Origen de los Indios de esta Provincia de Guatemala*.[36] The original manuscript later disappeared and only Ximénez' copy has survived. There have been various opinions about the probable author or authors of the *Popol Vuh* or rather who wrote down all these texts during the second half of the sixteenth century. Some attribute it to the Indian, Diego Reynoso, but according to Adrián Recinos, "so long as no new evidence is discovered which will throw light upon the matter, the famous manuscript must be considered as an anonymous account written by one or more descendants of the Quiché race according to the tradition of their forefathers."[37]

There are many studies and various editions of the *Popol Vuh*, including a rather inaccurate translation into French by the renowned French *abbé*, Charles Etienne Brasseur de Bourbourg. Among others who have worked with the manuscript are Karl Scherzer, Max Müller, H. Bancroft, Daniel G. Brinton, Francisco Pi y Margal, Georges Raynaud,

[35] See France V. Scholes and Ralph L. Roys, *The Maya Chontal Indians of Acalan-Tixchel*, 367–405.

[36] Adrián Recinos (tr.), *Popol Vuh*, 34–35.

[37] *Ibid.*, 29.

Miguel Angel Asturias, Antonio Villacorta, Leonhard Schultze-Jena, and more recently Adrián Recinos.[38] The ancient native-American bible has been translated into Spanish, French, German, English, and Japanese.

The *Popol Vuh* can be divided into a kind of introduction and four main sections. The introduction states the intention of covering everything which happened in the land of the Quichés and of revealing what was hidden about the origin of life and the beginning of history. It states that there was an ancient book which was concealed when the Spaniards came. In order not to forget the contents of this book, the author has set himself the task of writing down, "now in the days of the law of God and Christianity," this new *Popol Vuh*.

The first part deals with the cosmic origins, the different kinds of human beings created by the gods, and their successive destructions; there is also the story of two lesser gods, Hunahpú and Ixbalanqué, who were sent to earth to check the pride of Zipacná. The second part of the book contains other myths such as the one about the Ahup people who went to play ball with the lords of Xibalbá, the region of the dead, and the myth about the young girl, Ixquic, who became pregnant from the saliva which dripped from the skull of one of the lords who had been defeated in the ball game. The third and fourth sections record the history of the Quichés under their first four leaders: their pilgrimages, their efforts to gain possession of the fire, their rites and traditions, and the establishment and growth of the Quiché nation. The manuscript concludes with an appendix entitled *Papel del Origen de los Señores Quichés*.[39]

The *Título de los Señores de Totonicapán* was also written in the Quiché language, apparently around 1554. Although the author was influenced by Christian ideas and by those who imagined that the natives were descendants of the ten lost tribes of Israel, he also recorded genuine ancient chronicles and indigenous genealogy. Among other things, mention is made of the migration of the three nations or tribes of Quichés up to their arrival in Guatemala where they separated into different groups and of their organization, their struggles, the genealogy of various lords,

[38] *Ibid.*, 30–61.
[39] *Paper Concerning the Origin of the Lords* also appears in Recinos, *op cit.*, 237–39.

and the distribution of land. While much less detailed than the *Popol Vuh*, this manuscript confirms the information given in the sacred book of the Quichés. Unfortunately the original manuscript of the *Título de los Señores de Totonicapán* has disappeared, and all that remains is the Spanish translation prepared around 1834 by the parish priest of Sacapulas, Dionisio José Chonay, who seems to have had a thorough knowledge of the Quiché language.

The last of the three most important Quiché manuscripts is the *Rabinal Achí*, transcribed by the *abbé* Brasseur de Bourbourg in the village of Rabinal about 1856 with the assistance of the native elder Bartolo Ziz, who is said to have faithfully preserved the ancient Quiché text. The *Rabinal Achí*, or "The Lord of Rabinal," appears to be a native play in the pre-Hispanic form. The chapter devoted to ceremonies and theater will present it in the light of its literary value.

The Cakchiquels, another nation of the Maya family, have left evidence of their literature in the *Memorial de Sololá*, also known as *Anales de los Cakchiqueles* or *Memorial de Tecpan-Atitlán*. As were the books of *Chilam Balam*, it was transcribed by natives who knew the ancient traditions and told about "those who engendered men in ancient times, before these mountains and valleys were inhabited." It mentions the migration of the tribes; their passage through the great city of Tula and their arrival in what is today Guatemala. The accounts of migrations, the founding of cities, and struggles with the Quichés often show the style of epic poetry. The manuscript also mentions contacts between the Cakchiquels and the Spaniards who came to Guatemala under Don Pedro de Alvarado. As in the case of Náhuatl texts, it says of Alvarado's men, "the faces of the Spaniards were unfamiliar and the lords took them to be gods."

The *Memorial de Sololá* or *Anales de los Cakchiqueles*, sometimes also described as *Anales de los Xahil* because the authors belonged to this group of the Cakchiquels, describes the friars preaching Christianity, the rebellion of the natives, the acts of violence by Alvarado, the founding and destruction of the city of Guatemala, and the death of Doña Beatriz de la Cueva, wife of Alvarado. Some of the epic and historical passages, as well as a few short poems from this manuscript, will be analyzed later.

Among other documents in the Cakchiquel language is the *Historia de los Xpantzay de Tecpan Guatemala* and a text which Adrián Recinos has named *Guerras comunes de quichés y cakchiqueles* which deals with the wars between these Indian nations in pre-Hispanic days.

In addition to all these codices and documents in Náhuatl and in the Maya languages, something has to be said about the few literary creations that have survived from other ancient Mexican groups like the Otomís, the Tarascans, the Mixtecs, and Zapotecs.

The Otomís, with a language entirely different from Náhuatl, have lived for thousands of years in Central Mexico in contact with other cultures and peoples, among them the Toltecs and later the Tezcocans, Tlaxcalans, and Aztecs. Sometimes they joined the Náhuatl-speaking peoples and at other times were conquered by them. But under whatever conditions they lived, they always maintained their own individuality in spite of outside influences. Even today there are large groups of Otomís in several states of Central Mexico.

There are three main sources for the study of the Otomí productions. The previously described *Cantares Mexicanos* in the National Library of Mexico has a notation saying that it also includes "ancient songs of the native Otomís which were usually sung at feasts and marriages, now put down in the Náhuatl language with due consideration for the spirit of their song and the metaphorical images they used."[40] Several of these Otomí songs are real literary gems.

The other two manuscripts are pictorial codices at least partly copied from pre-Columbian sources. The *Códice de Huamantla* was painted on a large linen cloth of which six fragments are preserved in the National Museum of Mexico and three in the Humboldt Collection in Berlin. The *Códice Hueychiapan* contains an Otomí calendar and transcriptions of annals with explanations in the Otomí language.[41] Although neither of these two codices have been adequately analyzed nor the notations in Otomí entirely translated, it is certain that there are historical passages of literary value, especially in the *Hueychiapan*.[42]

[40] Fol. 6 r.

[41] Caso, *"Un Códice en Otomí,"* Proceedings of the XXIIIrd International Congress of Americanists.

The Tarascans, who in pre-Hispanic times inhabited a large part of what is today the state of Michoacán and some portions of the present states of Guanajuato, Querétaro, Guerrero, Colima, Jalisco, and Mexico, were a powerful nation never conquered by the Aztecs. Known also as the Purépechas, they spoke a language apparently unrelated to any other indigenous tongue. The culture of the Tarascans was, however, very similar to that found in the central region.

The little known about Tarascan literature comes from the sixteenth-century *Relación de Michoacán*. This important chronicle was written down verbatim by an anonymous missionary from accounts by Indian elders who had preserved the memory of their past. The anonymous missionary who gathered these materials at the request of the viceroy of New Spain, Don Antonio de Mendoza, clearly realized the significance of his work. In the introduction to the *Relación* he writes, "I serve only as interpreter for these elders and take into account that it is they who narrate." The chronicle was probably written down in 1538 or 1539 in Tzintzuntzan on the shores of Lake Pátzcuaro.[43] The arrangement of the materials presented is explained in the introduction. The first part tells of the principal gods and their feast days; the second describes how the Tarascans conquered and settled their lands; the third explains their system of government before the arrival of the Spaniards and the death of their lord, Caltzontzin. Unfortunately the first section is lost, but there are 264 pages of the other two parts. These contain color paintings in the old indigenous tradition. Paul Kirchoff, after a detailed analysis of the *Relación de Michoacán*, emphasized that "our text, not only in content but also in language, is undoubtedly the work of natives who dictated it to the friar. Furthermore, it can be said that at least two-thirds of the whole has the characteristic style of words fixed by tradition."[44] A few mythical and historical excerpts from this *Relación* will give some idea of Tarascan literature.[45]

[42] Pedro Carrasco Pizana in his study on the Otomí culture, *Los Otomíes*, discusses the notations concerning the calendar in this codex.

[43] Federico Gómez de Orozco, *Crónicas de Michoacán*, 6.

[44] In *Relación de Michoacán*, xx.

[45] Among the historical records of the Tarascans is the *Códice de Carapan*, also known as the *Códice Plancarte*.

The Mixtecs, in the present-day state of Oaxaca, are famous as artists and particularly as goldsmiths. They have left seven codices or painted books of historical and genealogical content. These pre-Hispanic manuscripts are undoubtedly one of the most important collections of ancient pre-Columbian painted books.[46]

Walter Lehmann and especially Alfonso Caso have done extremely valuable work on these codices, but even so they have not yet been entirely studied. Dr. Caso has published a detailed analysis of the genealogies contained in the *Codex Bodley*, the *Vindobonensis*, and the *Selden*.[47] Although these books appear to be schematic, they do have an extremely valuable series of historical records on which the pre-Hispanic Mixtecs based their oral traditions, legends, and accounts. Other investigators have gathered modern Mixtec texts containing legends and history in which there appears a certain continuity of tradition from generation to generation. Examples of this more recent literature are the Mixtec texts collected by Anne Dyck.

It only remains to add a few words about the testimonies left by the Zapotecs of Oaxaca whose inscriptions in stone have already been mentioned. The Zapotecs were close neighbors of the Mixtecs and they had very ancient forms of writing dating at least from the days of classic splendor. Unfortunately, little remains of their traditions and knowledge. However, in the General Archives of the Indies in Seville there has been a recent discovery of several booklets, dating from the early seventeenth century, which contain transcriptions dealing with ancient ceremonies connected with the astrological or ritualistic calendar.[48] Of a much later date is a beautiful legend in Zapotec taken down by Paul Radin in the village of Zaachila. It tells the story of the marriage of a

[46] These codices are known as the *Códices Becker*, Nos. 1 and 2, in the Museum of National History in Vienna; *Códice Bodley*, No. 2858, in the Bodleian Library of Oxford University; *Códice Colombino*, National Museum of Anthropology of Mexico; *Códice Nutall* and *Códice Selden*, Bodleian Library of Oxford University; and *Códice Vindobonense*, National Library of Vienna. In addition to these codices, there are also some post-Hispanic Mixtec manuscripts in which the indigenous techniques are also preserved. The principal ones are *Códice Dehesa*, *Códice Rickards*, *Códice Tulane*, and *Códice de Yanhuitlán*.

[47] *Interpretación del Códice Bodley 2858*. See also Philip Dark, *Mixtec Ethnohistory*.

[48] The texts included in these manuscripts have been discovered by Dr. José Alcina Franch, head of the Seminar of Americanist Studies of the University of Seville.

daughter of the Aztec king, Ahuítzotl, to the great Zapotec lord, Cosijoeza.

The descriptions of the texts preserved in Náhuatl, in the various Maya languages, and in Otomí, Tarascan, Mixtec, and Zapotec have already indicated the principal subjects found in native literatures: myths and legends, sacred hymns, various kinds of epic, lyric, and religious poetry, early forms of theater, chronicles and history, speeches and discourses, religious doctrines, and even the tenets of what may be called pre-Hispanic philosophy. There are also some works written down right after the Conquest which show the reaction of a conquered people through the eyes of those who witnessed and understood the destruction of their ancient culture and ways of life.

Náhuatl, Maya, and the other tongues provided not only an adequate but a rich and elegant medium for communication. By the juxtaposition of roots or morphemes and the use of a number of suffixes and prefixes, it was possible to express any idea with precision, however abstract and complex. The native wise men, "artists of the word," knew the literary possibilities of the language they spoke. In the case of the Aztecs, for example, their schools placed special importance on the art of fine speaking, the cultivation of *tecpillatolli*, the noble and precise form of expression.

The Náhuatl narrator or *tlaquetzqui*, the one who makes things stand out, followed a standard:

The narrator:
witty, he says things with spirit,
with lips and mouth of an artist.

The good narrator:
pleasing words, joyful words,
he has flowers on his lips.
His speech overflows with advice,
flowers come from his mouth.
His speech, pleasing and joyful as flowers;
from him come noble language
and careful sentences.

27

The bad narrator:
slovenly language,
he confuses words;
swallows them, speaks indistinctly.
He narrates awkwardly, describes things.
Says useless words,
he is without dignity.[49]

The good narrator was a true artist with his lips and mouth. He made an effort to use noble language and careful expression. It is emphasized that flowers came from his lips. Such metaphors, so frequent in American Indian languages, gave literary expression an unmistakable character. By using metaphors, by repeating the same idea twice in a different way, the ancient poets, speakers, historians, and wise men were able to draw extraordinary pictures. The abstract and the concrete appeared united, giving new life to myths and legends, history and doctrines.

The wise men of ancient Mexico held their literary works in such high esteem that they came to conceive a vision of life itself in poetic form, in terms of flower-and-song as they called it. Poets told of their anguish to discover a form capable of expressing their intuitions. For instance, the famous Ayocuan of Tecamachalco insisted that his songs came from the innermost heaven, but that in spite of his longing he was not able to express what he wished:

From within the heavens come
the beautiful flowers, the beautiful songs.
Our longing spoils them,
our expression makes them lose their fragrance.[50]

Inspiration and intuition, the longing to create, flower-and-song, or in other words metaphors and symbols, are at the heart of our native literatures. But rather than to try to reduce the various forms of expression to rules and principles, the reader is invited to discover for himself the rich human value of these literary creations. Many of them will be

[49] *Códice Matritense de la Real Academia*, fol. 122.
[50] *Cantares Mexicanos*, fol. 9 v.

studied in the following pages, those in Náhuatl translated directly by the author and those from other cultures taken from the works of researchers in the respective languages.[51]

[51] For those who wish to approach the texts in their original tongues, corresponding references appear in the bibliography.

I

Myths in Pre-Columbian Poetry

THE GREAT MYTHS told in Náhuatl and other native tongues are probably the oldest poetry of pre-Hispanic times. Similar legends often recorded in different languages suggest a common origin for the main cultures of Mesoamerica. For example, in Maya and Náhuatl literature there are accounts of the cosmic ages and the cultural hero Quetzalcóatl—Kukulcán of the Maya—as well as of the origin of maize. Indeed, a common thread runs through all the principal myths of ancient Mexico.

The creation of the world is described in the *Popol Vuh* of the Quichés, in the Maya *Chilam Balam of Chumayel*, and also in various Náhuatl texts, some of which were recounted to Sahagún by his native informants. They all relate the story of other ages or cosmological suns which succeeded each other before our present era. In these ages human beings were different, they were made of clay, of ashes, of wood, and finally of maize. Animals were different, as was sustenance which at first was very poor but improved in each successive age. According to some Náhuatl sources, there have been five ages ruled by the suns of water, earth, fire, wind, and movement. Other texts, the *Popol Vuh* and *Chilam Balam of Chumayel*, mention only four cosmic periods. In spite of this, they all agree on the idea of evolution toward better forms from age to age.

The *Popol Vuh*, as well as some Náhuatl manuscripts, attributes the original foundation of the world to a supreme dual principle, Our Mother–Our Father, which was the origin of everything which exists. This same idea appears in Mixtec codices and other documents of that culture. Later the Nahuas called this supreme Mother-Father dual prin-

30

ciple Ometéotl, which means God of Duality, the origin of all the other gods. In its masculine aspect Ometéotl engendered and in the feminine conceived all the cosmic forces which human beings called the innumerable gods of the four directions of the universe—rain, wind, fire, and the Region of the Dead.

Some of these gods, observing that four different times the universe had come to a violent end, wished to terminate this misfortune. They met in Teotihuacán and agreed to bring into being the fifth cosmic age which is the present. Thus the fifth age, called the Sun of Movement, was the result of the decision and voluntary sacrifice by the sons of the Dual God who threw themselves into a sacrificial fire. This blood sacrifice which brought into being the Sun and the Moon was the latent seed which much later ripened into a religious ritual for the Aztecs; if only the death of the gods could make possible the movement and life of the Sun, then only the sacrifice of men, who play the role of the gods on earth, can maintain its life and motion. Only in this way could they avoid a cataclysm which might bring an end to the Sun and the present age as those of ancient times had done.

These are some of the myths about the origin of the earth, the sun, and the moon as found in the first expressions of ancient Mexican epic poetry.

The principal character in the thought of ancient Mexico was Quetzalcóatl. Sometimes he was considered a god, an all-powerful divinity, and sometimes a culture hero, but he always played an extremely important part in all the ancient cultures.

Some Náhuatl myths attribute the origin of present-day human beings, as well as maize, to Quetzalcóatl. As a symbol of divine wisdom, Quetzalcóatl agreed to go to the Region of the Dead and search for the bones of men of other ages. Accompanied only by his *nahual*, a kind of double or alter ego, Quetzalcóatl descended to the world of the dead. There Mictlantecuhtli, Lord of the Region of the Dead, put him through a series of difficult tests. At last Quetzalcóatl gathered up the bones of a man and a woman and took them to a mythical spot called Tamoanchan. There the gods came together to grind up the bones in a very fine earthen tub, and Quetzalcóatl bled his male organ on them to impart life. Here once more blood sacrifice became the source of life and motion. Accord-

ing to the myth, the first humans were called *macehuales*, which meant
the indebted ones; they owed their existence in this fifth age to the sacrifice of Quetzalcóatl.

It was also Quetzalcóatl who was commissioned to go in search of
maize, the well-known American Indian grain. For this he went to the
red ant who lived near the Mountain of Our Sustenance where the maize
was hidden. Having changed himself into a black ant, he persuaded the
red ant, after much discussion, to let him take a few grains of maize. At
this point other gods appear in the myth. They are the *tlaloques* or gods
of rain who came from the four directions of the universe to fructify the
theft, making the maize grow on earth so that at last Quetzalcóatl might
bring the precious grain to men. The gods took some of the seeds,
masticated them, and put them into the mouths of the first human beings
so that they should be strong and live.

Along with the myths of Quetzalcóatl in the character of a god, there
are others in which he is the great priest of the Toltecs, the culture hero
of the pre-Columbian world. His reign is described as a life of abundance
with every kind of riches. The Toltecs received from him wisdom and
the arts. Quetzalcóatl, in fasting and chastity, lived in his palaces of
different colors which faced toward the four directions of the universe;
above all he was devoted to meditation and a search for new ways of
understanding divinity.

But this golden age of the Toltecs also came to an end, and Quetzalcóatl
had to flee to the east. Three wizards came to Tula to introduce the rites
of human sacrifice, and they overpowered the wise priest, confusing his
heart, and brought about his ruin. Since Quetzalcóatl appeared very old
and weak, the wizards showed him a mirror in which he saw himself
weighed down by the years. After a long conversation they persuaded
him to take an intoxicating drink which they said would cure him.
Quetzalcóatl, at first resisting, finally tasted the drink, drank all of it, and
became drunk. The wizards then began to practice witchcraft in Tula.
When Quetzalcóatl became conscious and realized what had happened,
he decided to go away to the region of light, the east, which is the land
of wisdom, of the black and the red.

Arriving at the edge of the sea on the coast of the Gulf of Mexico,

Quetzalcóatl disappeared. According to one version, he embarked on a magic raft of serpents; according to another, he cast himself into a great pyre and emerged as the morning star.

Quetzalcóatl as a culture hero is also found in the ancient Maya texts as Kukulcán and as Gucumatz among the Quichés. All these myths insist that even though Quetzalcóatl went away, he was to return. The god and the priest, often confused in native thinking, continued through the ages as symbol of the most lofty spiritual thought in ancient Mexico.

In addition to the myth of Quetzalcóatl, Náhuatl literature has poems about Huitzilopochtli and Coatlicue, patron deities of the Aztecs. The Quichés also have a myth which tells of lesser gods, Hunhunahpú and Wucubhunahpú. These gods were excellent ball players and the people of Xibalbá, the hidden country or Region of the Dead, heard about their games and were very displeased. Under pretext of wanting to compete with them, they persuaded the gods to come to Xibalbá. There Hunhun-ahpú was defeated and perished, and the people of Xibalbá put his skull up in the branches of a tree. One day a young girl named Ixquic came near the tree and heard Hunhunahpú's voice speak to her from the skull. Then suddenly she felt some drops of saliva fall on her hand from the fleshless head. The saliva impregnated Ixquic who gave birth to twins, the culture heroes Hunahpú and Ixbalanqué, who came to earth to humble the pride of Zipacná.

There are many texts telling about other lesser gods of rain, wind, and sowing and also popular beliefs about the beyond, the Region of the Dead, the nursing tree, paradise of the rain god, the heaven of the sun, directions of the universe, and celestial planes.

As a direct consequence of their mystico-militaristic thought, the Aztecs believed that everyone who died in battle became a follower of the Sun. Warriors, transformed into magnificent birds, accompanied the Sun in the morning; and women who died in childbirth, because they bore a man in combat, a prisoner in the womb, were also accepted among the followers of the Sun at dusk.

There were three other places in the beyond for special classes of people. Tlalocan, the mansion of Tláloc the rain god, was where those chosen by this god to die by drowning, to be struck by lightning, or to be afflicted with dropsy or gout found delight and happiness. Nearby was Chichihuacuauhco, place of the nursing tree; children who died before the age of reason gathered round this immense tree to drink the milk which dripped from its branches. And finally there was Mictlan, where most humans went, also known by other names expressing the Náhuatl idea: our-common-house, the-common-region-where-we-lose-ourselves, place-where-everyone-goes, place-where-we-exist-in-some-way, region-of-the-fleshless. According to some texts, those who went to Mictlan had to pass a series of trials before arriving at the end of their journey in the beyond; the tests lasted four years after which time the dead ceased entirely to exist. All these beliefs were part of the popular religion of the Nahuas.

In translation, the myths of pre-Columbian literature still show a characteristic strength of expression and color. The rhythmic style of many of these texts is similar to the mythical accounts and poems of other peoples and cultures. Their form of expression, which frequently repeats the same idea in parallel form, indicates that these texts were memorized in the pre-Hispanic centers of learning and recited during important religious festivals.

The myths show a concern for detail, expressing an idea from different angles. But along with this attention to detail, there also appears the concept of the whole within which small things become meaningful. What sometimes appear to be concrete details, such as flowers and song, quetzal plumage, or jade and precious stones, are metaphors used to express the most subtle and beautiful abstractions. Thus the mythical poems of the Nahuas and the Mayas point to the mysterious realm of the gods and lay the foundation for a doctrine of the world, man, and his existence in an art which joins the concrete and abstract, the real and the fantastic.

Perhaps the oldest myth of the Nahuas is the one which tells about cosmic origin. They believed that the earth was founded many thousands of years ago and that four suns or ages have existed before the present era. During these ages there has been an evolution in spiral form, and each successive age has brought better elements, plants, and human beings.

The first men were made of ashes; water washed them away and they

34

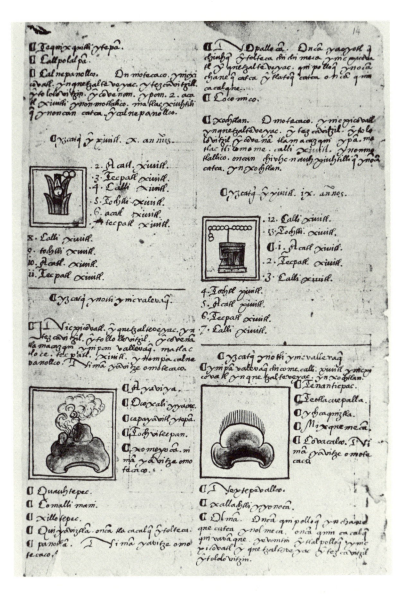

A page of the *Historia Tolteca-Chichimeca* (*Annals of Cuauhtinchan*), 14.

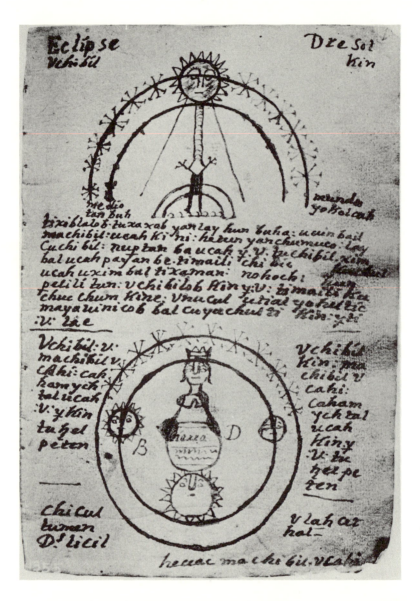

A page from the Maya manuscript of the *Book of Chilam Balam of Chumayel.*

became fish. In the second age the earth was inhabited by giants, but in spite of their size they were weak and tigers devoured them. The men of the third age also came to a tragic end; they were changed into turkeys. Those who lived in the fourth era or sun were eventually carried away by the wind and became what the ancient texts call monkey-men. The fifth or present age originated in Teotihuacán. This is the age of Quetzalcóatl, the priest and prince of Tula.

One of the clearest expressions of this myth in the Náhuatl language is found at the beginning of the ancient manuscript known as *Anales de Cuauhtitlán*:

Thus it is told, it is said:
there have already been four manifestations
and this one is the fifth age.

So the old ones knew this,
that in the year 1-Rabbit
heaven and earth were founded.
And they knew this,
that when heaven and earth were founded
there had already been four kinds of men,
four kinds of manifestations.
Also they knew that each of these
had existed in a Sun, an age.

And they said of the first men,
their god made them, fashioned them of ashes.
This they attributed to the god Quetzalcóatl,
whose sign is 7-Wind,
he made them, he invented them.
The first Sun or age which was founded,
its sign was 4-Water,
it was called the Sun of Water.
Then it happened
that water carried away everything.
The people were changed into fish.

Then the second Sun or age was founded.
Its sign was 4-Tiger.

It was called the Sun of Tiger.
Then it happened
that the sky was crushed,
the Sun did not follow its course.
When the Sun arrived at midday,
immediately it was night
and when it became dark,
tigers ate the people.
In this Sun giants lived.
The old ones said
the giants greeted each other thus:
"Do not fall down," for whoever falls,
he falls forever.

Then the third Sun was founded.
Its sign was 4-Rain-of-Fire.
It happened then that fire rained down,
those who lived there were burned.
And then sand rained down.
And they say that then
it rained down the little stones we see,
that the *tezontle* stone boiled
and the big rocks became red.

Its sign was 4-Wind,
when the fourth Sun was founded.
It was called the Sun of Wind.
Then everything was carried away by the wind.
People were turned into monkeys.
They were scattered over the mountains,
and the monkey-men lived there.

The fifth Sun,
4-Movement its sign.
It is called the Sun of Movement
because it moves, follows its course.
And the old ones go about saying,
now there will be earthquakes,
there will be hunger

and thus we will perish.
In the year 13-Reed,
they say it came into existence,
the sun which now exists was born.
That was when there was light,
when dawn came,
the Sun of Movement which now exists.
4-Movement is its sign.
This is the fifth Sun which was founded,
in it there will be earthquakes,
in it there will be hunger.[1]

This Sun, its name 4-Movement,
this is our Sun,
in which we now live,
and this is its sign,
where the Sun fell in fire
on the divine hearth,
there in Teotihuacán.
Also this was the Sun
of our prince of Tula,
of Quetzalcóatl.[2]

During the age of the Fifth Sun, which began in Teotihuacán, the gods decided to establish a new race of humans on earth. They entrusted the restoration of man to Quetzalcóatl, and for this purpose he went to Mictlan, the land of the dead, in search of the precious bones with which to form the new men. Mictlantecuhtli, Lord of the Region of the Dead, was reluctant to give up the bones and tried to prevent Quetzalcóatl from carrying away the remains of the past generations. But assisted by his double or *nahual* and also by the worms and hornets, Quetzalcóatl succeeded in taking possession of the bones and carrying them to Tamoanchan, the place-of-our-origin. There, with the aid of the goddess Quilaztli, the bones were ground up and put in a fine earthen tub. Then Quet-

---

[1] *Anales de Cuauhtitlán*, fol. 2

[2] *Manuscript of 1558*, also known as *Legend of the Suns*, fol. 77. Included as an appendix to the text of *Anales de Cuauhtitlán*.

zalcóatl, by bleeding his male member over the bones, infused life into them:

And as soon as the gods came together
they said: "Who shall live on the earth?
The sky has already been established,
and the earth has been established.
But who shall live on the earth, oh gods?"
Citlalinicue, Citlaltónac,
Apantecuhtli, Tepanquizqui,
Quetzalcóatl, and Tezcatlipoca
were grieved.

Then Quetzalcóatl went to Mictlan,
he approached Mictlantecuhtli and Mictlancíhuatl
and immediately said to them:
"I have come for the precious bones
which you keep here,
I have come to take them."
And Mictlantecuhtli said to him:
"What would you do with them, Quetzalcóatl?"
And Quetzalcóatl answered him:
"The gods are concerned
that someone shall live on the earth."
And Mictlantecuhtli replied:
"Very well. Sound my conch shell
and go four times around my domain."

But the conch shell had no holes;
therefore Quetzalcóatl called the worms;
they made holes in it and
then the bees and hornets went inside
and made it sound.
On hearing it sound, Mictlantecuhtli said again:
"Very well. Take the bones."
But Mictlantecuhtli said to those who served him:
"People of Mictlan!
Oh gods, tell Quetzalcóatl
he must not take them."

Quetzalcóatl replied:
"Indeed, yes, I take possession of them."
And he said to his *nahual* [alter ego],
"You go and tell Mictlantecuhtli I will not take them."
And his *nahual* said loudly, "I will not take them."

But then Quetzalcóatl went,
he gathered up the precious bones.
The bones of the man were together on one side
and the bones of the woman together on the other side
and Quetzalcóatl took them
and made a bundle.
Again Mictlantecuhtli said to those who served him:
"Gods, is Quetzalcóatl
really carrying away the precious bones?
Gods, go and dig a big hole."
They went and dug it.
And Quetzalcóatl stumbled, frightened by quail,
and fell into the hole.
He fell down as if dead
and the precious bones were scattered,
so that the quail chewed and gnawed upon them.

After a while Quetzalcóatl was revived,
he was grieved, and he said to his *nahual*:
"What shall I do now?"
His *nahual* answered him:
"Although the affair has started badly,
let it continue as best it may."
Quetzalcóatl gathered up the bones,
put them together, made again a bundle,
and carried them to Tamoanchan.
As soon as he arrived,
the goddess called Quilaztli,
also called Cihuacóatl,
ground them up
and put them in a fine earthen tub.
Quetzalcóatl bled his male organ on them.
And immediately the gods named

Apantecuhtli, Huictolinqui, Tepanquizqui,
Tlallamánac, Tzontémoc,
and the sixth, Quetzalcóatl,
all did penance.
And they said:
"Oh gods, the *macehuales* are born."
And thus we mortals owe our life to penance,
because for our sake the gods did penance.[3]

This fragment is only one example of the great quantity of myths about Quetzalcóatl, the god, wisdom of the supreme divinity, restorer of men, and discoverer of maize.

There is a legendary story about a Toltec culture hero, Our Prince Quetzalcóatl, the priest who was named for the god. The following texts, taken from the *Anales de Cuauhtitlán* and the *Códice Florentino*, are in the style of an epic poem telling of the deeds and accomplishments of Quetzalcóatl, the priest, the inventor of the arts, the great spiritual leader of the Toltecs:

The Toltecs, the people of Quetzalcóatl,
were very skillful.

Nothing was difficult for them to do.
They cut precious stones,
wrought gold,
and made many works of art
and marvelous ornaments of feathers.
Truly they were skillful.

All the arts of the Toltecs,
their knowledge, everything came from Quetzalcóatl.

The Toltecs were very wealthy,
their foodstuffs, their sustenance, cost nothing.
They say that the squash
were big and heavy.
That the ears of corn
were big and heavy as the pestle of a *metate* [grinding stone].

3 *Manuscript of 1558*, fol. 75–76.

40

And the blades of amaranth,
like palm leaves,
you could step on them,
climb on them.

Also they grew cotton
of many colors:
red, yellow, pink,
purple, green, bluish green,
blue, light green,
orange, brown, and dark gold.
These were the colors of the cotton itself.
It grew that way from the earth,
no one colored it.
And also they raised there
fowl of rare plumage:
small birds the color of turquoise,
some with green feathers,
with yellow, with flame-colored breasts.
Every kind of fowl
that sang beautifully,
like those that warble in the mountains. . . .

And those Toltecs were very rich,
they were very happy;
there was no poverty or sadness.
Nothing was lacking in their houses,
there was no hunger among them. . . .

They say that when Quetzalcóatl lived there,
often the wizards tried to trick him
into offering human sacrifices,
into sacrificing men.
But he never did, because he loved his people
who were the Toltecs. . . .

And they say, they relate,
that this angered the magicians
so that they began to scoff at him,
to make fun of him.

The magicians and wizards said
they wanted to torment him
so that finally he would go away,
as it really happened.

In the year 1-Reed, Quetzalcóatl died,
truly they say
that he went to die there,
in the Land of the Black and Red Color.

They say that in the year 1-Reed
he set himself on fire and burned himself;
they call it the burning place,
where Quetzalcóatl sacrificed himself.
And they say that when he was burned,
immediately his ashes rose up,
and all the exquisite birds came to see:
those which flew about in the heavens,
the macaw, the blue bird,
the sunflower bird, the red and blue bird,
the golden yellow one, and other birds of fine plumage.

When the pyre had ceased to burn,
Quetzalcóatl's heart came forth,
went up to heaven, and entered there.
And the ancient ones say
it was converted into the morning star. . . .[4]

The Aztecs preserved this and other legends about the Toltec priest, Quetzalcóatl. But they also cherished as their exclusive possession myths about their tribal god, the young warrior Huitzilopochtli. This poem gives the account of his birth and early adventures. It tells of his miraculous conception from a ball of fine feathers which entered the womb of the goddess Coatlicue, who was to be his mother.

Coatlicue's other children, Coyolxauhqui and the four hundred gods of the south, seeing that she was with child, were very annoyed. They considered it a dishonor and tried to kill Coatlicue. But Huitzilopochtli spoke to his mother from within her womb, saying, "Do not be afraid; I know

[4] *Códice Matritense del Real Palacio*, fol. 132 v.– 134 v., and *Anales de Cuauhtitlán*, fol. 7.

what I must do." Exactly at the moment when the four hundred gods of the south, led by Coyolxauhqui, advanced to kill Coatlicue, Huitzilopochtli was born. Immediately he attired himself with the insignia of a warrior; he cut off Coyolxauhqui's head and overpowered her brothers, the four hundred gods.

From that very moment Huitzilopochtli took possession of their gear, their ornaments, and their destiny. In this way, according to the myth, the Aztec god was born and with him his fame as lord of war. This legend, completely different from those of Toltec origin, reflects the mentality of the Aztecs, who were obsessed by a mystico-militaristic concept of life. The forceful expression of the poem resembles other works of Aztec art, for example, the extraordinary sculpture of Coatlicue, mother of Huitzolopochtli, now in the National Museum of Anthropology in Mexico City. It is hardly necessary to mention that the Aztecs found in this myth a source of inspiration for their spirit of conquest and domination.

The Aztecs greatly revered Huitzilopochtli;
they knew his origin, his beginning,
was in this manner:

In Coatepec, on the way to Tula,
there was living,
there dwelt a woman
by the name of Coatlicue.
She was mother of the four hundred gods of the south
and their sister
by name Coyolxauhqui.

And this Coatlicue did penance there,
she swept, it was her task to sweep,
thus she did penance
in Coatepec, the Mountain of the Serpent.
And one day,
when Coatlicue was sweeping,
there fell on her some plumage,
a ball of fine feathers.
Immediately Coatlicue picked them up

and put them in her bosom.
When she finished sweeping,
she looked for the feathers
she had put in her bosom,
but she found nothing there.
At that moment Coatlicue was with child.

The four hundred gods of the south,
seeing their mother was with child,
were very annoyed and said:
"Who has done this to you?
Who has made you with child?
This insults us, dishonors us."
And their sister Coyolxauhqui
said to them:
"My brothers, she has dishonored us,
we must kill our mother,
the wicked woman who is now with child.
Who gave her what she carries in her womb?"

When Coatlicue learned of this,
she was very frightened,
she was very sad.
But her son Huitzilopochtli, in her womb,
comforted her, said to her:
"Do not be afraid,
I know what I must do."
Coatlicue, having heard
the words of her son,
was consoled,
her heart was quiet,
she felt at peace.

But meanwhile the four hundred gods of the south
came together to take a decision,
and together they decided
to kill their mother,
because she had disgraced them.
They were very angry,

they were very agitated,
as if the heart had gone out of them.
Coyolxauhqui incited them,
she inflamed the anger of her brothers,
so that they should kill her mother.
And the four hundred gods
made ready,
they attired themselves as for war.

And those four hundred gods of the south
were like captains;
they twisted and bound up their hair
as warriors arrange their long hair.
But one of them called Cuahuitlícac
broke his word.
What the four hundred said,
he went immediately to tell,
he went and revealed it to Huitzilopochtli.
And Huitzilopochtli replied to him:
"Take care, be watchful,
my uncle, for I know well what I must do."

And when finally they came to an agreement,
the four hundred gods were determined
to kill, to do away with their mother;
then they began to prepare,
Coyolxauhqui directing them.
They were very robust, well equipped,
adorned as for war,
they distributed among themselves their paper garb,
the *anecúyotl* [the girdle], the nettles,
the streamers of colored paper;
they tied little bells on the calves of their legs,
the bells called *oyohualli*.
Their arrows had barbed points.

Then they began to move,
they went in order, in line,
in orderly squadrons,

45

Coyolxauhqui led them.
But Cuahuitlícac went immediately up onto the mountain,
so as to speak from there to Huitzilopochtli;
he said to him:
"Now they are coming."
Huitzilopochtli replied to him:
"Look carefully which way they are coming."
Then Cuahuitlícac said:
"Now they are coming through Tzompantitlan."
And again Huitzilopochtli said to him:
"Where are they coming now?"
Cuahuitlícac replied to him:
"Now they are coming through Coaxalpan."
And once more Huitzilopochtli asked Cuahuitlícac:
"Look carefully which way they are coming."
Immediately Cuahuitlícac answered him:
"Now they are coming up the side of the mountain."
And yet again Huitzilopochtli said to him:
"Look carefully which way they are coming."
Then Cuahuitlícac said to him:
"Now they are on the top, they are here,
Coyolxauhqui is leading them."

At that moment Huitzilopochtli was born,
he put on his gear,
his shield of eagle feathers,
his darts, his blue dart-thrower,
called the turquoise dart-thrower.
He painted his face
with diagonal stripes,
in the color called "child's paint."
On his head he arranged fine plumage,
he put on his earplugs.
And on his left foot, which was withered,
he wore a sandal covered with feathers,
and his legs and his arms
were painted blue.

And the so-called Tochancalqui
set fire to the serpent of candlewood,
the one called Xiuhcóatl
that obeyed Huitzilopochtli.
With the serpent of fire he struck Coyolxauhqui,
he cut off her head,
and left it lying there
on the slope of Coatépetl.
The body of Coyolxauhqui
went rolling down the hill,
it fell to pieces,
in different places fell her hands,
her legs, her body.

Then Huitzilopochtli was proud,
he pursued the four hundred gods of the south,
he chased them, drove them off
the top of Coatépetl, the mountain of the snake.
And when he followed them
down to the foot of the mountain,
he pursued them, he chased them like rabbits,
all around the mountain.
He made them run around it four times.
In vain they tried to rally against him,
in vain they turned to attack him,
rattling their bells
and clashing their shields.
Nothing could they do,
nothing could they gain,
with nothing could they defend themselves.
Huitzilopochtli chased them, he drove them away,
he humbled them, he destroyed them, he annihilated them.

Even then he did not leave them,
but continued to pursue them,
and they begged him repeatedly, they said to him:
"It is enough!"

But Huitzilopochtli was not satisfied,

47

with force he pushed against them,
he pursued them.
Only a very few were able to escape him,
escape from his reach.
They went toward the south,
and because they went toward the south,
they are called gods of the south.
And when Huitzilopochtli had killed them,
when he had given vent to his wrath,
he stripped off their gear,
their ornaments, their *anecúyotl*;
he put them on, he took possession of them,
he introduced them into his destiny,
he made them his own insignia.

And this Huitzilopochtli, as they say,
was a prodigy,
because only from fine plumage,
which fell into the womb of his mother, Coatlicue,
was he conceived,
he never had any father.
The Aztecs venerated him,
they made sacrifices to him,
honored and served him.
And Huitzilopochtli rewarded
those who did this.
And his cult came from there,
from Coatepec, the Mountain of the Serpent,
as it was practiced from most ancient times.[5]

Maya literature has a different quality. The delicate sensitivity of the
Mayas shows from the very beginning in their poems and legends. Reading their myths today evokes an image of an old Maya inscription on a
stele or in the interior of one of the palaces which still remain from this
ancient culture. From the wealth of Maya myths, three are unusually
expressive. The first is from the "Book of the Ancient Gods" in *Chilam*

---

[5] *Florentine Codex*, Book III, Chapter I.

Balam of Chumayel and is an account of "the history of this earth." Although similar to Náhuatl poems of the ages or cosmological suns, the myth has its own distinctive flavor which might be described as a mystical approach to the realm of the gods and ultimate reality.

It was in the 11-Ahau Katún,
[during the eleventh period of twenty years]
when there appeared those who had great power
to hoodwink the thirteen gods of the heavens.
Their names were not known. . . .
It was the time
when the earth had just awakened.
They did not know what would happen.

The thirteen gods of the heavens were seized
by the nine gods of the underworld.
It rained fire, it rained ashes;
trees and stones fell over.
The trees struck against each other
and the stones against other stones.

Seized were the thirteen gods,
with their heads battered,
faces bashed in,
and skin broken out;
they were bent over at the shoulders.
They were deprived of their great serpent,
with the bells on its tail,
also the plumage of quetzal was taken away.

They partook of ground beans,
together with the seed of the serpent,
together with its heart,
ground seeds of squash,
big ground seeds of squash
and ground kidney beans.
He who has no limit, nor end,
wrapped up everything and tied it together
and went to the thirteenth heavenly plane.

Then the skin of the serpent fell off
and pieces of its bones
fell here on the earth.
Then its heart escaped;
the thirteen gods did not want
their heart and their seed to escape.
The orphans, the forsaken ones and the widows,
those not strong enough to live,
were killed with arrows.
They were buried in the sand at the shore
of the sea, in the waves.
Then in a great sheet of water the waves came.
When the great serpent was taken away,
the heavens fell
and the earth was submerged.

Then the four gods,
the four Bacabs destroyed everything.
And when the destruction was finished,
they remained firmly in their places,
to ordain the dark-reddish men.
Then rose up the first white tree in the north.
Rose up the arch of the heavens,
symbol of destruction beneath.
After the first white tree was set up,
then rose up the first black tree,
on it perched the bird with the black breast.
Then rose up the first yellow tree,
and as symbol of destruction beneath
was perched the bird with the yellow breast.
The steps of the dark-reddish men were heard,
those of the dark-reddish countenance.
And then rose up the green tree of abundance,
in the center of the world,
in memory of the earth's destruction. . . .

At that time Uuc Cheknal,
he who fertilizes the maize seven times,
came down from the seventh plane of the heavens.

C· Vacah. ok qutal voa rubanic yuhuh, ok xcamelic nichhal vinack
chuvach huyu, xax rah Enzat chic nhauh voo caok chuvach huyu.

O chi belehe ah xelvoohunarubanic yuhuh.

O vakaki ah xeluvakak yuhuh.

O chi oxi ah. xel ruvukhuna yuhuh.

C· Chupam ruvah xak huna yuhuh xcam chic qutuhila, rumaah
xe ynup, xepalica, xeyaar vi chicomic, xhak can çak bin ah mak
chiox lahuh ah mak.

O chi oxlahuh ah. xel vah xaka yuhuh.

O chi lahuh ah. xel rubeleh huna.

C· Cablauhah oktel lauha yuhuh ok xigo pokob, cak cha quel ru-
ma nhauh hamama oxlahuh ģij, hi ħiħ chinima Sokal xban
xul ronohal vu hamas chi y ximchee, chivah xaħi ymox xban

O chi vuku ah. rulauha rubanic yuhuh.

O cahi ah. xel ruhu lauha.

O chi ħun ah. rucablauha.

O chi hu lahuh ah gnxel roxlauha yuhuh. ah perģil

C· Oxlahuh giquin xcam xosohaah voo queh rix hay lah lahuh vdua
rugnhol gi kab, angahula chic matul cah lauha yuhuh ok rome
nhauh ox lahuh ģij, hamama chio xiah mak xcam nhauh ħi
ħiħ.

51

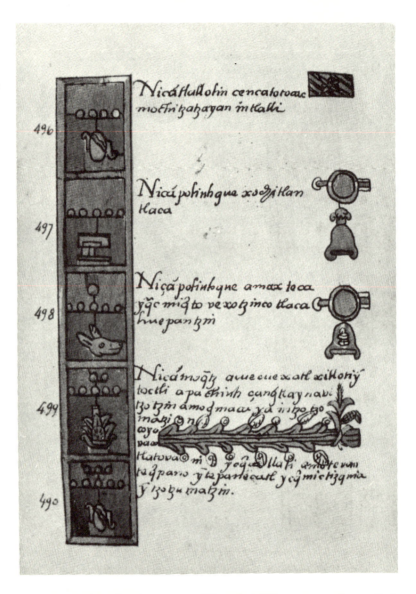

Aztec annals for the years 4-Flint to 8-Flint, a page from *Codex Aubin*.

Coming down, he stepped on the shoulders of Itzamá,
he came while the earth and the heavens were being cleansed.

He walked along the fourth canopy of stars.
The earth was not yet lighted.
There was no sun,
there was no night, there was no moon.
They would awaken
when the earth awakened.
Then the earth awoke.
Many eons of time
after the earth awoke,
finally it dawned for them.

The kingdom of the second term was declared
the kingdom of the third term.
Then the thirteen gods began to weep.
In this age they wept.
All became red....
Then the foundation of the red age was established....[6]

The innate exuberance of Maya thinking shows plainly in the above
text. Their epic account of the cosmic cataclysms and struggles among
the gods certainly has a parallel in the sacred poems of the Náhuatl-
speaking groups of ancient Mexico. But since these texts of the later
Maya wisdom in Yucatán have a unique combination of mysticism and
a delicate but forceful expression, they contrast sharply with the more
factual accounts of the Aztecs.

The Quichés of Guatemala, also Maya in language and culture, have
recorded their own myths about the origin of the world, the gods, and
the various cosmic ages in the extraordinary *Popol Vuh* or sacred book
of the people. An example of their epic accounts is the Quiché version of
what happened to the first men of the present cosmic age when the
gods realized the intelligence and ability with which these mortals were
endowed. This unusually beautiful myth of universal significance reminds us of legends from other cultures:

[6] Ralph L. Roys (ed.), *Chilam Balam of Chumayel*, 99–102. Original Maya text, 32.

These are the names
of the first men who were created and formed:
the first man was Balam-Quitzé,
the second was Balam-Acab,
the third Mahucutah, and the fourth Iqui-Balam.
These are the names
of our first mothers and fathers.
They say that they were only made and formed,
they had no mother, they had no father.
They were called simply human beings.
They were not born of woman,
They were not begotten
by the Creator and the Former,
by the Forefathers.
Only by a prodigy, by a work of magic
were they created and formed
by the Creator and the Former,
the Forefathers Tepeu and Gucumatz.

Since they had the appearance of men,
they were men;
they spoke, conversed,
they saw and heard,
they walked, they took hold of things.
They were good and handsome men.
Their figure was that of human beings.

They were endowed with intelligence,
they saw and instantly their vision was extended,
they were able to see,
to know everything there was in the world.
When they looked,
at once they saw their surroundings
and observed round about them
the arch of the heavens and the surface of the earth.
They saw all the hidden things,
without having to move. . . .
Great was their wisdom,
their sight reached to the woods,

the rocks, the lakes, the seas,
the mountains, and the valleys.
Truly they were remarkable men,
Balam-Quitzé, Balam-Acab, Mahucutah, and Iqui-Balam. . . .
But the Creator and the Former
saw this with displeasure.
"It is not right, the way our creatures talk,
our handiwork.
They know everything, the large and the small."
Thus they spoke and again took counsel together.
"Now what will we do with them?
Their sight should reach only
to what is near,
they should see only a little of the surface of the earth!
It is not right, the way they talk.
Are they not simply our creatures, our workmanship?
Must they be gods as well,
when it dawns, when the sun comes out?
And if they procreate and multiply?
And if they propagate?"
Thus they spoke.

"We must curb their desires,
for what we see is not right.
Perchance should they become equal with us,
their creators,
who are able to encompass great distances,
who see and know all?"

This they said, the Heart of Heaven,
Huracán, Chipi-Caculhá.
Raxa-Caculhá,
Tepeu, Gucumatz, the forefathers,
Ixpiyacoc, Ixmucane, the Creator and the Former.
Thus they spoke and immediately
they changed the nature of their handiwork,
of their creatures.

Then the Heart of Heaven
threw a vapor over the eyes of the men,

their eyes were clouded
as when one breathes on a mirror.
Their eyes were covered
so they could only see what was near,
only that was clear to them.

Thus their wisdom was destroyed
and all the knowledge of the four men,
the origin and beginning of the Quichés.[7]

One more example also taken from the *Popol Vuh* tells of some of the ancient Quiché culture heroes. It relates how the fleshless skull of Hunhunahpú spoke and with saliva impregnated the young girl Ixquic, who gave birth to the hero Hunahpú. The complete story, with its many dialogues, rich in metaphor, is one of the masterpieces of pre-Hispanic literature:

"All is well," the skull said to the young girl,
"reach out here with your right hand."
"Yes," the girl replied
and lifted her right hand,
reached it up toward the skull.

Then the skull ejected a bit of saliva,
it fell on the palm of the young girl's hand.

She looked carefully at her hand,
but the saliva from the skull
was no longer in her hand.

"In my saliva and in my spittle
I have given you my offspring,"
said the voice of the skull.
"Now nothing is left in my head,
it is only a skull without flesh.
Thus become the heads of great princes,
only the flesh makes them appear handsome.

---

[7] Recinos (ed.), *Popol Vuh: The Sacred Book of the Ancient Quiché Maya*, 167–69. Original Quiché text, *Popol Vuh: Das Heilige Buch der Quiché Indianer von Guatemala*, 100–104.

When they die, men marvel
at the bones.
So also is the nature of children,
they are as saliva and spittle,
even though they be children of a lord,
of a wise man or master of the word.
Their nature is not lost when they go away;
it is inherited.
It does not end, nor disappear, the image of a lord,
of a wise man or a master of the word.
They leave it to their daughters,
and to the sons they conceive.
This is what I have done to you.
Come to the surface of the earth,
you will not die.
Believe in my words,
for thus it shall be,"
said the head of Hunhunahpú.[8]

These texts are only a sample of the rich treasure of myths and legends left by two of the better known nations in ancient Mexico: the Nahuas, including the Aztecs, and the Maya and Quiché groups in Yucatán and what is today Guatemala.

The Mixtecs of Oaxaca were famous as architects, goldsmiths, and potters. One of their myths tells of their beliefs about the origin of the world and men. The original in the Mixtec tongue is no longer in existence, but Fray Gregorio García made a transcription of the old text preserved by a vicar in the monastery of Cuilapa. The vicar took his material from various indigenous codices and the oral testimony of Mixtec sages. This account again shows the rhythm of expression in parallel phrases, describing the same idea with different shades of meaning, which are evidence of its native origin.

In the year and in the day
of obscurity and utter darkness,
before there were days and years,

8 *Ibid.*, 119–20. Original Quiché text, 46–48.

the world being in deep obscurity,
when all was chaos and confusion,
the earth was covered with water,
there was only mud and slime
on the surface of the earth.
At that time ...
there became visible
a god who had the name 1-Deer
and the surname Snake of the Lion
and a goddess, very genteel and beautiful,
whose name was also 1-Deer
and whose surname was Snake of the Tiger.
These two gods are said to have been the beginning
of all the other gods. . . .
As soon as these two gods became
visible on the earth, in human form,
the accounts of our people relate
that with their power and wisdom,
they made and established a large stone,
on which they built
a very sumptuous mansion,
constructed with the finest workmanship,
which was their seat and residence on earth.
And on top of the highest part
of the house and habitation of these gods
was a copper ax,
the blade turned upward,
above which were the heavens.
This large stone and the mansion
were on a very high hill,
near the village of Apoala. . . .
This large stone was named
"the-place-where-the-heavens-were."
And there they remained many centuries
in complete tranquility and contentment,
as in a pleasant and delightful place,
the world being
at that time in obscurity.

And these gods,
father and mother of all the gods,
while in their mansion,
had two male children, very handsome,
prudent and wise in all the arts.
The first was called
Wind-of-Nine-Snakes,
taken from the name of the day he was born.
The second was called
Wind-of-Nine-Caverns,
which also was the name
of the day he was born.
These two children
were raised in great luxury.
The elder, when he wanted to amuse himself,
turned into an eagle,
which flew up very high.
The second transformed himself into a small animal,
in form of a serpent with wings,
which flew through the air
with such nimbleness and cunning,
that he passed through large stones and walls,
and he made himself invisible. . . .
The two brothers, for their pleasure,
planted a garden;
they put there many kinds of trees,
flowers and roses
and trees with fruit
and many herbs.
After all this
began the creation of the heavens and the earth. . . .
Men were restored to life
and in this way
began the Mixtec kingdom. . . .[9]

The fragmentary account of the divine origins as recalled by the Mix-

[9] Text preserved by the Vicar of Cuilapa and included in Fray Gregorio García, *Origen de los Indios del Nuevo Mundo e Indias Occidentales*, 137.

tecs gives at least a glimpse into their most ancient form of literary expression. Probably, as in the case of Nahua and Maya cultures, some of their poems were conceived well in advance of the first painted books. The rhythm and forceful expression suggest they were preserved in the hearts and minds of the people.

These ancient myths, like those in China, India, and the Near East, were without any definitive author. They were the result of the accumulated wisdom of the elders who sought meaning and roots in a world where everything changes and in which nature, sickness, and death threaten constantly. They were an attempt to explain things, the world and the mysteries of life.

The similarities found in the myths of different cultures of ancient Mexico lead to the belief that they were all inherited from an even more ancient people, creators of a remote mother culture. But along with the obvious similarities in the legends, there are also differences. To give an example, the myth of Huitzilopochtli and Coatlicue, exclusive to the Aztecs, offers a key to the very essence of their thinking and explains the ideals and rituals of the People of the Sun. The Toltecs, led by Quetzalcóatl, had followed the path of art and spirituality in order to survive the threatened end of this sun or the present age; they believed that each man must overcome death by himself and make the journey to the region of wisdom, Tlilan-Tlapalan, the Land of Black and Red Color, just as Quetzalcóatl had done. The Aztecs, on the contrary, undertook to prevent the death of the sun by offering precious liquid, the blood of the victims who were obtained by continuous conquests which extended the dominions of Huitzilopochtli to the four corners of the world.

The study of pre-Columbian myths opens the door to the minds of these peoples. In the myths is the seed of what was to become their religious thought; recited during festivals and ceremonies or sung to the accompaniment of flutes, conch-shells, and drums, they were also the beginning of religious drama.

To the contemporary philosopher, psychologist, and anthropologist these myths offer an unlimited field for research, for they contain the earliest expressions of the native world view, the original feelings and aspirations of the people, and the foundation of many of their future institutions and ways of life. This brief chapter has presented only a few of the great myths which escaped oblivion. Anyone approaching them in their original tongue will find a key to the understanding of the symbols and magic of the universe in which the ancient Mexicans lived.

II

The Sacred Hymns

CLOSELY RELATED TO EPIC POETRY telling of cosmic origins and great deeds of the gods and the culture heroes are the sacred hymns found in the literatures of ancient Mexico. The hymns were chanted in honor of the gods, especially at great religious ceremonies. Some were in the form of entreaty directed to the god of rain, the gods of corn, and even the god of war; others expressed thanks for benefits received; and there were hymns of praise in which both priests and people recalled the attributes of divinity. Most of the extant sacred hymns, some of which are very ancient, come from Náhuatl-speaking people. The Mayas and others such as the Mixtecs and Zapotecs also had this form of religious expression during their days of splendor, but unfortunately the greater part of these ancient texts was lost in the days following the Conquest.

The hymns in this chapter are probably the most lofty expressions of religious belief among the ancient Mexicans. Some of their concepts, the rhythm and parallelism of phrases, and the forceful metaphors remind us of invocations and hymns of other cultures, for instance those of the Rig-Veda written in Sanskrit. In fact, Daniel G. Brinton, a North American who was one of the first researchers to study and translate some of these early Mexican texts, gave his anthology of pre-Columbian hymns the unexpected title of *Rig-Veda Americanus.*

The modern student and translator of these hymns faces many problems. For instance, obscurities arising from the archaic language in which the hymns are expressed, not to mention the concepts themselves, derived from an entirely different religious world view.

Dr. Angel María Garibay K., in a special work on some of these hymns, wrote: "No translation of any text, whatever 'the language or culture, and especially ancient texts, pretends to eliminate the problem of obscurity which is inherent in the work itself. It is impossible to make the Hebrew psalms or the Vedic hymns as clear as an article in the morning paper. Transcriptions which eliminate all obscurity are suspect. The differences in time, ways of thinking, and nuances of the language make it impossible to translate any text completely. The most any translator can hope for is not to be too disloyal to his text."[1]

Hymns preserved in the Náhuatl language have obviously come down to us through the Aztecs and their neighbors who lived at the time of the Conquest. Nevertheless, because of their style and the ideas expressed, different periods of composition can be distinguished. Often the key is within the text itself where the native compiler has made a comment about its origin. This is the case with some of the hymns from the collection gathered by the Indian informants of Bernardino de Sahagún, who recorded the hymns recited by Nahua wise men in the region of Tezcoco and Mexico-Tenochtitlan.

Two poems will be quoted here from the few which seem to be most ancient. They may even have been included in that famous book of the gods which Ixtlilxóchitl mentions, the *Teoamoxtli* or "divine book" of the Toltecs. Actually they come to us in two documents of different origin, the *Historia Tolteca-Chichimeca* and the *Madrid Codex*.

In the *Madrid Codex*, where the native wise men recall what they knew about their cultural origins and mention Teotihuacán, the City of the Gods, there is a brief poem which they say used to be sung at that city in the presence of those who had died before they were cremated. This hymn declares that death is transformation. Men are changed into flame-colored pheasants and women into owls. They are deified in the beyond, in the paradise of the rain god of which there is a remarkable mural painting in one of the palaces at Teotihuacán. Only a few lines remain from the ancient poem. It invokes the coming of dawn as the beginning of a new life, while birds of many colors fly about in a heaven suffused with light. Transcribed here is the hymn along with the words which accompany it in the text:

[1] *Veinte Himnos Sacros de los Nahuas,* 26.

Thus the dead were addressed,
when they died.
If it was a man, they spoke to him,
invoked him as a divine being,
in the name of pheasant;
if it was a woman, in the name of owl;
and they said to them:

"Awaken, already the sky is tinged with red,
already the dawn has come,
already the flame-colored pheasants are singing,
the fire-colored swallows,
already butterflies are on the wing."

For this reason the ancient ones said,
he who has died, he becomes a god.
They said: "He became a god there,"
which means that he died.[2]

The other ancient hymn is found in the *Historia Tolteca-Chichimeca*. According to the Náhuatl account, two Toltec chieftains are at the entrance of a cave hidden in a hill. They have come to invite a group of Chichimecs to join them. From inside the cave the Chichimecs ask their visitors to identify themselves as true Toltecs with a song. The two chieftains then chant one of their ancient hymns in honor of Ometéotl, the supreme God of Duality. In the hymn they declare that Ometéotl is the source of power, the mirror that makes things show forth, the inventor of men. The text, worded in an archaic language, suggests considerable antiquity:

In the place of authority,
in the place of authority we command;
it is the mandate of our Principal Lord,
Mirror which makes things show forth.
They are already on the way, they are prepared.
Intoxicate yourselves, intoxicate yourselves,
the God of Duality is acting,

2 *Códice Matritense de la Real Academia*, fol. 195 r.

the Inventor of Men,
Mirror which makes things show forth.[3]

This firmly rooted faith in a supreme god of duality, also mentioned in the myths, appears in another hymn, perhaps as ancient as that in the Toltec-Chichimec history. It is included in one of the famous *huehuetlatolli* or "discourses of the elders" collected by Sahagún. Here Ometéotl is invoked in his primal function as "mother and father of the gods," omnipresent and eternal:

Mother of the Gods, Father of the Gods,
the Old God,
distended in the navel of the earth,
engaged in the enclosure of turquoise.
He who dwells in waters the color of the bluebird,
He who dwells in the clouds,
the Old God,
He who inhabits the shadows of the region of the dead,
the Lord of fire and of the year.[4]

Still in use in Aztec days, but of great antiquity, were the twenty sacred hymns given to Sahagún by the native informants at Tepepulco in the present-day state of Hidalgo. According to these informants, they were sung at ritual feasts in honor of the gods. The singing of these hymns accompanied by music, ceremonies, and sacrifices marks the actual beginning of drama in the Náhuatl world. Of the three presented here, the first is a song to Ixcozauhqui, Lord of the Yellow Face, one aspect of the fire god and probably the most ancient divinity worshiped in all of pre-Columbian Mexico. The hymn mentions definite places, such as Tzonimolco, which was the name of a building dedicated to this god in the main temple of Mexico-Tenochtitlan. There was a school in this building whose pupils collected the wood for the sacrifices. Other ceremonies took place there, including the relighting of the fire. The hymn mentions two more names: Tetemocan, meaning "where different things come down,"

[3] *Historia Tolteca-Chichimeca*, facsimile edition in *Corpus Codicum Americanorum Medii Aevi*, I, 33.

[4] *Códice Florentino*, Book VI, fol. 34 r.

63

and Macatlan, another building in the temple where priests practiced the flute and other musical instruments.

The main idea of the hymn is to incite the priests to the cult of the gods, especially the fire sacrifice in honor of the sun. The rhythm and parallelism is obvious as an indication that the poems were learned by heart. The people as well as the priests chanted them during important ceremonies.

In Tzonimolco, my fathers,
may you not be ashamed.
In Tetemocan, my fathers,
may you not be ashamed.
Oh, in Macatlan, my lords,
the drums of Chicueyocan are resounding.
House of magicians, the magician descends.
In Tzonimolco there is singing; we have begun.
In Tzonimolco there is singing; we have begun.
Behold, it is time to go out with masks.
Behold, it is time to go out with masks.
In Tzonimolco . . . a man
is about to be offered!
Oh, the Sun has come out; oh, the Sun has come out,
that a man may be offered to him!
In Tzonimolco the song of the servants
resounds again and again:
"With deeds the princes enrich themselves,
make themselves worthy of glory."
Oh Little Mother, call together the people;
you who inhabit the House of Mist, the House of Rains;
call together the people.[5]

One of the most important hymns in the Aztec religious cult was the song to Huitzilopochtli. The son of Coatlicue, identified with the sun and divine warrior par excellence, had become the supreme god in the minds of the people. The wise men and priests obviously had not forgotten Ometéotl, the God of Duality, Master of the Close and Near. The popular pre-eminence of Huitzilopochtli as patron deity of the Aztecs

[5] Garibay K., *Veinte Himnos Sacros de los Nahuas*, 85.

simply means that his cult had become enormously important. It is well known that the main temple in Tenochtitlan was dedicated to him and to Tláloc, the rain god.

The hymn to the young warrior was probably chanted in the form of a dialogue. In the first two lines a singer refers to Huitzilopochtli, who is identified with the sun and follows its path in the heavens. Then Huitzilopochtli replies, in the voice of the chorus, saying that it is he who has made the sun appear. Again the voice of the singer exalts the magnificent one who inhabits the region of the clouds. The last part, again chanted by the people, praises the god and ends with warlike exclamations. As already mentioned, this is also another example of the beginnings of later drama, which culminated in what may be called the perpetual theater of the Nahuas, with performances and sacrifices throughout the year which coincided with different religious festivals.

Huitzilopochtli, the young warrior,
he who acts above, moving along his way.

"Not in vain did I take the raiment of yellow plumage,
for it is I who made the Sun appear."

Portentous one, who inhabits the region of clouds,
you have but one foot!
Inhabiter of the cold region of wings,
you have opened your hand!

Near the wall of the region that burns,
feathers come forth.
The Sun spreads out,
there is a war cry....
My god is called Protector of Men.
Oh, now he advances, comes well adorned with paper,
he who inhabits the region that burns,
in the dust, in the dust, he gyrates.

Our enemies are those of Amantla;
come adhere to us!
War is made with combat,
come adhere to us!

65

Our enemies are those of Pipiltlan:
come adhere to us!
War is made with combat,
come adhere to us![6]

One more example from the series of twenty sacred hymns is a song in honor of the mother goddess in her aspect as patron of the day 7-Serpent. This is a brief poem of only two stanzas in which the goddess is petitioned, invoked by her name of Seven Cobs of Corn, to protect the crops. Repeatedly the song begs her to awaken and rise up, for she is Our Mother. If she goes away, men remain orphans. But if she goes to Tlalocan, the house of Tláloc, the rain god, she can intercede for good crops. This is a fine example of the simplicity of this ancient literary form:

Oh Seven Cobs of Corn ... arise now,
awaken.... You are Our Mother!
You would leave us orphans;
go now to your house, Tlalocan.

Oh Seven Cobs of Corn ... arise now,
awaken.... You are Our Mother!
You would leave us orphans;
go now to your house, Tlalocan.[7]

The following songs of later origin, probably during the second half of the fifteenth century, are more personal in nature. They are the work of wise men such as the famous lord, Nezahualcóyotl of Tezcoco, and others who had meditated profoundly on the mystery of deity. The first of these texts, taken from a Náhuatl manuscript in the Latin American Collection at the University of Texas, is a hymn to the Giver of Life. The ancient wise man is seeking "the house of the One Who Invents Himself." He searches for Tloque Nahuaque, Master of the Close and the Near, as he would seek someone among the flowers. Flowers and songs, as we have seen, are symbolic of poetry and art in indigenous thinking. The wise men of ancient Mexico believed that in order to find the Giver of Life, he must be approached through art.

[6] *Ibid.*, 31.
[7] *Ibid.*, 187.

In no place can be the house of He who invents Himself,
In no place can be the house of He who invents Himself,
but in all places He is venerated.
His glory, His majesty is sought throughout the earth.

It is He who invents things,
it is He who invents Himself: God.
In all places He is invoked,
in all places He is venerated.
His glory, His majesty is sought throughout the earth.

No one here is able,
no one is able to be intimate
with the Giver of Life;
only is He invoked,
at His side,
near to Him,
one can live on the earth.

He who finds Him,
knows only one thing: He is invoked,
at His side near to Him,
one can live on the earth.

In truth no one
is intimate with You,
oh Giver of Life!
Only as among the flowers
we might seek someone,
thus we seek You,
we who live on the earth,
we who are at Your side.

Your heart will be troubled
only for a short time,
we will be near You and at Your side.

The Giver of Life enrages us,
He intoxicates us here.
No one is at His side
to be famous, to rule on earth.

Only You change things
as our heart well knows;
no one is at His side
to be famous, to rule on earth.[8]

The second text, here named "Beginning and End," tells how divinity creates things. "With flowers and songs He paints and shades, as if writing a codex, and in this way He creates all that exists." But the Giver of Life is also he who brings an end to existence. Man lives in his painted books but some day will be erased from them. Again the ancient wise man uses the symbolism of flower and song to say something about the beginning and the end of existence:

With flowers you write,
Oh Giver of Life!
With songs you give color,
with songs you shade
those who must live on the earth.

Later you will destroy
eagles and tigers;
we live only in your painting
here, on the earth.

With black ink you will blot out
all that was friendship,
brotherhood, nobility.

You give shading
to those who must live on the earth.

Later You will destroy
eagles and tigers;
we live only in your painting
here, on the earth.[9]

A last example of Náhuatl sacred poems is actually a series of questions concerning the reality of man's existence in relation to He Who is the

---

[8] MSS *Romances de los Señores de la Nueva España* (Collection of Náhuatl songs and poems preserved at the Library of the University of Texas), fol. 4 v.–5 v.

[9] *Ibid.*, fol. 35 r.

Inventor of Himself. For the native thinker, "no one can know completely the richness and the flowers of the Giver of Life." Nor can man know whether there will be existence in the place of mystery. He begins to doubt, but finally extricates himself from the uncertainty by taking refuge once more in the symbolism of art. Thanks to this, at least here on earth he can exist.

> Do men have roots, are they real?
> No one can know completely
> what is Your richness, what are Your flowers,
> oh Inventor of Yourself!
> We leave things unfinished.
> For this I weep,
> I lament.
> Here with flowers I interweave my friends.
> Let us rejoice!
> Our common house is the earth.
> In the place of mystery, beyond,
> is it also like this?
> Truly, it is not the same.
> On earth: flowers and songs.
> Let us live here![10]

Just as with their ancient myths, the Maya sacred hymns also show certain similarities in comparison with texts of the Nahuas. The probable explanation is that there had been many contacts between the two cultures ever since the Teotihuacán period and especially in Toltec days when Nahuas migrated southward. But unfortunately the Mayas did not have a Sahagún or a team of well-trained Indian scholars who devoted their time to collecting and preserving the old texts and traditions.

It is a tragedy that Fray Diego de Landa destroyed codices and other sources of information in Yucatán. But at least it can be said in his favor that later he seemed to regret this and wrote down his *Relación* describing the calendar and ancient customs, and mentioning particularly the festivals and religious formalities during which priests and people chanted sacred hymns. But few of these Maya hymns remain, and even

[10] *Ibid.*, fol. 41 v.

those few have come to us by chance. Some are included in the famous books of *Chilam Balam*, transcribed in among chronicles, prophecies, and myths. Some others of a later origin are recorded in a recently published Maya manuscript under the title *The Book of the Songs of Dzitbalché*. Finally, mention should be made of the hymns transcribed at the beginning of this century by A. M. Tozzer from the oral tradition of the Lacandon Indians. It is known that this Maya group, living in isolation on the banks of the Usumacinta River (between Chiapas and Guatemala), has managed to preserve many of its old customs and beliefs.

What remains of the sacred literature of the Mayas confirms what has already been said about their myths. Here, too, is the same refined, aesthetic sensitivity with great depth of thought. The frequent metaphors, the colored silk-cotton trees, the pheasants and turkeys with yellow crests, and the flints, fruits, and many-colored seeds show the atmosphere of exuberance in which the Maya people lived.

This first hymn praises the gods of the four quarters of the universe. It reads like a commentary on the brilliantly colored pages of an old Maya codex as it describes the gods of the four directions and their attributes:

The red flint
is the sacred stone
of Ah Chac Mucen Cab
[the red spirit hidden in the earth].
The red mother silk-cotton tree
is his arbor in the east,
the red *chacalpucté* is also his tree,
the red *zapote* and the red mushrooms....
The red turkeys with the yellow crest
are his turkeys.
The light brown and red maize are his maize.

The white flint
is the sacred stone of the north.
The white mother silk-cotton tree
is the arbor of the white Mucen Cab
[the white spirit hidden in the earth].
The white turkeys are his turkeys.

The white beans are his beans,
The white maize is his maize.

The black flint
is the stone of the west.
The black mother silk-cotton tree
is his arbor.
The purple and black maize is his maize.
The yam with the black stalk is his yam.
The black turkeys are his turkeys.
The black maize is his living maize.
The black kidney bean is his kidney bean.
The black bean is his bean.

The yellow flint
is the stone of the south.
The yellow mother silk-cotton tree
is his arbor.
The yellow *pucté* is his tree.
Yellow is his yam.
The yellow maize is his living maize.
The kidney bean with the yellow shoulder
is his kidney bean.[11]

Other similar compositions which vividly portray the symbolism of the deities of the four cosmic directions are also found in the *Chilam Balam* books. Some even may have been inscribed on the steles or in the few remaining codices which cannot be deciphered until the key to ancient Maya writing is discovered.

The following Maya religious hymn comes from the above mentioned *The Book of the Songs of Dzitbalché*. It is the "Song of the Bowman's Dance" which was probably chanted during the celebration of the sacrifice by arrows. The victim was tied to a stake placed up on a kind of stage. The people gathered round it, and a priest gave the signal to begin the dance and the song. Several warriors with their bows and arrows began to dance round the victim. Synchronized with the song and the

[11] Roys, *Chilam Balam of Chumayel*, 64–65. Original Maya text, 15–16.

music, they shot arrows at the one to be sacrificed. The victim's blood dropped on the ground, symbolizing fertilization of the earth.

This sacrifice may be revolting to our contemporary way of thinking, but at least we can understand its deep symbolism. Sacrifice, for the Mayas and other people of ancient Mexico, was a tribute which had to be paid to the gods. The world was restored and men brought back into existence by divine sacrifice, by the blood of the gods. In order to preserve the universe, it was necessary to offer continuously to divinity the precious liquid which maintains life. Thus, in the bowman's dance blood fertilizes the earth:

Oh watcher, watcher from the trees,
with one, with two,
we go to hunt at the edge of the grove,
in a lively dance up to three.
Raise your head high,
do not mistake,
instruct well your eyes
to gather the prize.

Make sharp the tip of your arrow,
make taut the cord
of your bow; now you have good
resin of *catsim* on the feathers
at the end of the arrow's rod.
You have rubbed well
the fat of a male deer
on your biceps, on your muscles,
on your knees, on your twin muscles,
on your shoulders, on your chest.

Go nimbly three times round
about the painted stone column,
where stands that virile lad,
unstained, undefiled, a man.
Go once, on the second round
take up your bow, put in the arrow,
point it at his chest; you need not
use all your strength

so as to kill him,
or wound him deeply.
Let him suffer
little by little,
as He wishes it,
the magnificent Lord God.

The next time you go round
this stony blue column, the next time
you go round, shoot another arrow.
This you must do without
stopping your dance, because
thus it is done by well-bred
men, fighters, those who
are sought after, pleasing
in the eyes of the Lord God.

And as the Sun appears
over the forest to the east,
the song of the bowman begins.
These well-bred men, fighters,
do their utmost.[12]

This song, which accompanied the sacrifice, was actually the recollection and staging of the old myth which forever links the idea of fertility and the renewal of life with the necessity for a blood offering.

Of later origin are the sacred poems belonging to the Lacandons, the small Maya group which has lived for centuries in isolation and still survives. The song presented here was until recently chanted by them in honor of the gods while they burned incense in a brazier. During the celebration of this ceremony, *pozol*, or sour dough of maize mixed with water, was distributed among those present. The fact that up to recent days this text survived among this Maya group shows how deeply rooted the old traditions were.

In front of you I offer my copal [incense],
it is for you.

[12] Barrera Vásquez (ed.), *El Libro de los Cantares de Dzitbalché*, 77–78.

Offered to the father, it is for you,
raised up to the father.
I fulfill again my offering of *pozol* for you, for you,
offered to the father.
I fulfill again my offering of *pozol* for you, for you.
In front of you I make once more my gift,
for your blessedness.
I offer it so that my gift shall not be stale,
it shall remain sound,
it shall be the head [principal part] of my gift, for you.
It must not fail, the gift I make you!
It must not break, the gift I make you!
See me making my gift to you, oh father!
That I may not be overcome by the fire of fever!
You are in front of the new brazier,
see me making once more a gift to you for your blessedness,
see me making a gift to you for the spirit of my children.
That sickness shall not come near them.
That the cold wind shall not imprison their feet.
That the fire of fever shall not imprison them.
Enter, go and look on my child,
make safe my child.[13]

These hymns are only an example of the rich religious expression of the Mayas. Together with the Náhuatl texts they testify to the existence of a sacred literature in pre-Columbian Mexico. According to the testimony of some of the chroniclers, the Mixtecs and Zapotecs of Oaxaca, the Tarascans of Michoacán, and others also sang hymns of praise and entreaty to their gods during religious festivals and ceremonies. But unfortunately these hymns were never transcribed, and with only a few fragments of late origin, little can be said about them.

The importance the ancient Mexicans gave to these forms of honoring and praising their gods is well illustrated in the Book of the People, the *Popol Vuh* of the Quiché Mayas. In the recalling of the successive creations of humans, there is a statement that the gods were concerned to create man in order to have someone who would invoke them, who

---

[13] A Lacandon sacred song, in Alfred M. Tozzer, *A Maya Grammar*, 118–19.

74

would praise them. The first men, made of earth and lacking intelligence, could not chant hymns to the gods. It was much the same with those made of wood; they "did not remember the Heart of the Heavens ... did not think about the Creator and the Former." And precisely because human beings of earlier ages did not invoke the gods, they were destroyed. Only men of the present age, who raise their voices to the heavens, will be able to multiply and populate the earth. In this myth the *Popol Vuh* includes the ancient hymn chanted by mortals, the forefathers of the Quichés, in order to please the supreme divinity:

> Oh You, Tzacol, Bitol, Creator, Former,
> look upon us, hear us!
> Do not leave us, do not forsake us.
> Oh God, Who is in heaven and on earth,
> Heart of the Heavens, Heart of the Earth!
> Give us our offspring,
> our issue,
> may the Sun move along and give light.
> May it dawn, may the light come!
> Give us many good roads,
> level roads.
> May the people be at peace,
> enjoy a long peace;
> and make them prosperous,
> give us a good life and useful existence.[14]

By invoking the gods, human beings will continue to exist. With this in mind, pre-Columbian wise men searched for the most beautiful words with which to give form and meaning to their sacred hymns.

[14] *Popol Vuh: The Sacred Book of the Ancient Quiché Maya*, 173.

III
Lyric Poetry

THE OLD CHRONICLES frequently mention lyric poetry and songs, especially those composed in the Náhuatl and Maya tongues. Although here also much has been lost, this form of verse in which poets expressed their own ideas and feelings, often closely related to religious celebrations and festivals, is one of the forms of literature from which the greatest number of works have survived.

This is especially true of Náhuatl lyric poetry. There are three main collections of songs preserved in the National Library of Mexico, the library at the University of Texas, and the National Library of Paris. From the Mayas comes *The Book of the Songs of Dzitbalché* and also some poems scattered through the various books of *Chilam Balam* as well as in the *Popol Vuh* of the Quichés. Very few lyric compositions from the other cultures of ancient Mexico have come down to us although mention can be made of some Otomí poems of pre-Hispanic origin.

Before approaching this lyric poetry, it will be helpful to analyze some of the most frequent stylistic procedures. These were more or less alike in all the various early Mexican literatures and show a certain similarity to the forms of expression used in other ancient compositions also preserved by an unbroken tradition, as in the case of the Bible and other texts from the Eastern cultures.

Anyone who reads indigenous poetry cannot fail to notice the repetition of ideas and the expression of sentiment in parallel form. Sometimes a thought will be complemented or emphasized through the use of different metaphors which arouse the same intuitive feeling, or two phrases will present the same idea in opposite form. A few examples will make this clear. In an Aztec poem which exalts the Sun, Huitzilopochtli, who is invoked by priests and people alike, the same thought is expressed twice:

> From where the eagles are resting,
> from where the tigers are exalted....

And the parallelism reappears in the same poem singing the greatness of Mexico-Tenochtitlan:

> Who could conquer Tenochtitlan?
> Who could shake the foundation of heaven?

In the following lines parallelism reinforces a single idea. The Aztecs are not afraid to die in war, because—

> This is our glory,
> this is Your command....[1]

Another device used in lyric poetry, as well as in discourses and other forms of composition, consists of uniting two words which also complement each other, either because they are synonymns or because they evoke a third idea, usually a metaphor. This particular stratagem is seldom found in Indo-European languages, but is very common in Mexican indigenous tongues, especially Náhuatl. Examples of this are the following: flower-and-song which metaphorically means poetry, art, and symbolism; skirt-and-blouse which implies woman in her sexual aspect; seat-and-mat which suggests the idea of authority and power; face-and-heart which means personality. It is not difficult to imagine the many possibilities of this idiomatic device, especially when used so frequently in lyric poetry. Metaphor thus becomes a permanent part of expression.

Other stylistic procedures in this native poetry are a kind of recurring phrase, used to impress the main idea on the mind of he who reads or listens, and the "key words," another expedient often adopted in indigenous poems though not exclusive to poetry. The latter consists of the repetition of the same word to evoke the same metaphor, thus giving unity to the poem. These and other stylistic resources give indigenous lyric poetry its unique character. This is especially true of Náhuatl poetry, considered here in greater detail.

[1] *Cantares Mexicanos*, fol. 19 v.

77

There are several hundred lyric poems preserved in the Náhuatl manuscripts already mentioned. Although they are often anonymous, the names of some of the most famous poets are known. Among them were the kings of Tezcoco, Nezahualcóyotl and his son Nezahualpilli; the lord Tecayehuatzin of Huexotzinco; Prince Ayocuan of Tecamachalco; and some others.

The subject matter of their poems may appear rather limited at first sight. The principal themes were the meditations of the wise men concerning divinity and the beyond, the pleasure of conversing with friends, the mystery of death, recollections of princes and elders, adventures in war, love for women and children, and even some purely erotic poems. Most of these compositions were recited or sung at festivals and reunions, accompanied by flutes and drums, the so-called *huéhuetl* and *teponaztli*. In some cases they appear to be the forerunners of a very ancient form of dramatic presentation, with groups of singers carrying on a chanted dialogue among themselves. Other poems that are more profound apparently were recited only in gatherings of wise men and poets.

That this type of poetry was highly esteemed by ancient Mexicans is shown by the fact that there were special groups of priests and elders who were responsible for teaching the songs carefully and also for examining and approving new compositions. The priests who taught were called *tlapizcatzitzin* or "conservators," and the *Códice Matritense* comments on their duties:

> The conservator had charge of songs composed in honor of the gods, all the divine hymns. In order that no one should make a mistake, he took the greatest care in teaching the divine songs to people in all parts of the town. A public crier would announce a meeting of the people so they could learn the songs well.[2]

The priests of Epcohua, the Mother-of-Pearl Serpent which was one of the titles of Tláloc, the rain god, were responsible for giving an opinion on new hymns and songs:

> The duty of the shaved priest of Epcohua Tepictoton was the following: he decided about the songs. When someone composed a song, he was in-

[2] *Códice Matritense del Real Palacio*, fol. 259 r.

formed so that the song could be presented; he gave orders to the singers, and they went to sing at his house. When anyone composed a song, he gave his opinion about it.[3]

The various examples presented here from the many Náhuatl poems and songs are grouped according to subject matter. Among the ancient songs there are many compositions exalting friendship. Most of these were recited or sung at gatherings of wise men and *cuicapicque* or "forgers of songs." Three of them are translated from the manuscript now in the Latin American Collection at the University of Texas. Two are almost certainly from the region of Tezcoco, and the other, attributed to Temilotzin, is Aztec.

"Friendship on Earth" is an appropriate title for the first. It expresses two main ideas: friendship, to know each other's faces, is one of the pleasures during the brief span of life and if we sing flower songs together, our words will live on earth after we have gone away. A mutual sadness helped composers to understand, and furthermore is what makes songs endure forever:

> Let us have friends here!
> It is the time to know our faces.
> Only with flowers
> can our song enrapture.
> We will have gone to His house,
> but our word
> shall live here on earth.
> We will go, leaving behind
> our grief, our song.
> For this will be known,
> the song shall remain real.
> We will have gone to His house,
> but our word
> shall live here on earth.[4]

"Song of Brotherhood" expresses a yearning to find the way of befriending the community and all humankind. With necklaces, with

3 *Ibid.*, fol. 260 r.
4 *MSS Romances de los Señores de la Nueva España*, fol. 27 v.

macaw feathers, with circlets of song, the poet encompasses those who are his friends, trying to give them whatever he has. A singer believes that this is the most he can do while on earth, until the day comes when all will have to go to the region of mystery:

> I am come, oh my friends,
> with necklaces I entwine you,
> with feathers of the macaw I adorn you,
> a precious bird, I dress with feathers,
> I paint with gold,
> I embrace mankind.
> With trembling quetzal feathers,
> with circlets of song,
> I give myself to the community.
> I will carry you with me to the palace
> where we all,
> someday,
> all must betake ourselves,
> to the region of the dead.
> Our life has only been loaned to us![5]

"Temilotzin's Poem" was composed a few years before the Spanish Conquest by a noble Aztec warrior, a tiger knight who fought the Spaniards and was with Cuauhtémoc when Tenochtitlan fell. According to the *Anales de Tlatelolco*, he preferred to kill himself rather than surrender. Temilotzin, who understood the message of flower-and-song, wrote that he was a messenger of God, a poet who had come to earth transformed into a poem in order to make friends here. His verse shows that even among Aztec warriors there were artists and wise men.

> I am come too,
> here I am standing;
> now I am going to forge songs,
> make a stem flowering with songs,
> oh my friends!
> God has sent me as a messenger.
> I am transformed into a poem,

[5] *Ibid.*, fol. 2 r.

I, Temilotzin.
I am come, too,
to make friends here.[6]

The friendship of wise men and poets, recorded in poems such as these, also found expression in reunions where the forgers of songs presented their works. In one of these meetings of poets and elders the subject under discussion was the true meaning of poetry. This reunion probably took place around the year 1490. Masters of the spoken word from various places came together at the house of the lord Tecayehuatzin, prince of Huexotzinco. The guests reclined on mats in the shade of large *ahuehuete* trees in an orchard near the home of their host, Tecayehuatzin. As was customary, servants passed tobacco and large cups of foaming chocolate.

The discussion, preserved in an old Náhuatl manuscript now in the National Library, begins with a greeting by the host, Tecayehuatzin, who expresses a desire to know the real meaning of flower-and-song, poetry, art, and symbolism. He asks about the origin of flowers and songs. Is it possible to say true words on earth, he asks, or is it man's destiny to search continuously, sometimes thinking he has found what he yearns for, but in the end going his way and leaving behind only the memory of his songs?

Tecayehuatzin's questions receive a wide variety of answers. One by one the guests express their ideas. The elder, Ayocuan, believes that art and symbolism are gifts from the gods, but he doubts what today would be called their transcendental value. Ayocuan does not know if flowers and songs survive in the beyond, in the world where they say we exist after death, our-common-house-where-we-lose-ourselves. These are his words:

Will I have to go like the flowers that perish?
Will nothing remain of my name?
Nothing of my fame here on earth?
At least my flowers, at least my songs!
Earth is the region of the fleeting moment.
Is it also thus in the place
where in some way one lives?

[6] *Loc. cit.*

81

Is there joy there, is there friendship?
Or is it only here on earth
we come to know our faces?[7]

Aquiauhtzin, a poet from Ayapanco, gives poetry his own personal meaning. He avoids the question of survival of art, symbolism, and poetry by saying that for him flowers and songs are the way in which to invoke the supreme Giver of Life, who sometimes makes Himself known through art and symbolism. But in most cases, Aquiauhtzin concludes, one can only say that we search for Him among the flowers, as one would search for a friend.

Cuauhtencoztli, another poet whose depth of thought marks him as a native philosopher, doubts the reality of art, because he doubts that man has roots on earth:

I, Cuauhtencoztli, here I am suffering.
What is, perchance, true?
Will my song still be real tomorrow?
Are men perhaps real?
What is it that will survive?
Here we live, here we stay,
but we are destitute, oh my friends![8]

Tecayehuatzin and other poet friends answer Cuauhtecoztli, trying to overcome what they consider a pessimistic attitude. Only flowers and songs, art, and symbolism can overcome sadness; they are man's riches and joy on earth.

The discussion, which so far has described poetry and art as a gift of the gods, as the survival of man on earth, a way to discover divinity, a possible wealth for mankind, now takes a different direction. The lord Xayacamach of Tlaxcala suggests that flower-and-song, poetry, and art, like the hallucinatory mushrooms, are the best means of intoxicating the heart and forgetting our sadness. Those who eat mushrooms in religious gatherings see marvelous visions, ephemeral forms of many colors, more real than reality itself. But afterwards this fantastic world fades like a

[7] *Cantares Mexicanos*, fol. 10 r.

[8] *Ibid.*, fol. 11 r.

dream, leaving man weary and empty. For Xayacamach this is art and symbolism, flowers and songs.

Other opinions are expressed. One poet says that he only gathers flowers to cover his cottage, close by the house of the paintings. As the discussion is about to end, the host, Prince Tecayehuatzin, speaks once more. He continues to believe that flower-and-song is the only way in which to say true words on earth. But since he realizes that not everyone has accepted his view, he suggests one last idea, with which all can agree: that flower-and-song, poetry, and art make possible the reunion of friends. These are his words:

> Now, oh friends,
> listen to the words of a dream:
> each spring brings us life,
> the golden corn refreshes us,
> the pink corn makes us a necklace.
> At least this we know:
> the hearts of our friends are true![9]

The words spoken by Tecayehuatzin and his poet friends show the variety of opinions in the pre-Hispanic world about the real meaning of art. They also show that wise men were trying to find an aesthetic concept as a basis for their vocation of creating flowers and songs. Obviously it was the existence of countless poems, discourses, and narratives which made possible the discussion about flower-and-song; the answers given in the above dialogue take for granted the reality of individual and personal experience and the valuable intuitive truths discovered by reflection. These had to be communicated, even if it required a great deal of effort to find a way of arousing in others what one's own heart had felt in solitary intuition.

There is also ample proof in the codices and Náhuatl poetry that the ancient Mexicans gave considerable thought to death. In popular religious thinking, especially in Aztec days, there are many references to death in battle, death of the victims who were sacrificed, and a possible death of everything that exists in the fifth age or Sun which will end violently, just as the previous ages described in early myths.

[9] *Ibid.*, fol. 11 v.

In the texts and painted books there are descriptions of Mictlan, the Region of the Dead, known also as the place-of-the-fleshless (Ximoayan) and our-common-place-where-we-lose-ourselves (Tocempopolihuiyan). Also mentioned are Tlalocan as the paradise of Tláloc, where those who are chosen by the rain god go; the Heaven of the Sun (Tonatiuhilhuícac) for those who die in war or sacrifice and are changed into companions of the Sun; and, of course, the place-of-the-nursing-tree (Chichihua-quauhco) where newborn infants go in the other world.

But in contrast to these religious ideas about death, which may be considered orthodox in ancient Mexico, there are texts—especially poems —with more personal ideas on the significance of the beyond and the inevitable end of life on earth. The following three poems each convey a different opinion about death.

The first, here entitled "Love And Death," appears to be a conversation with the beloved. The poet begs the one he loves to bring her heart close to him. But at the same time, in apparent contradiction, he recognizes that the closeness of this human love torments him; the fear of losing it reminds him of death. He repeats over and over that in the end he will have to go away; he cannot escape death. This idea brings him to realize that even the deepest love must come to an end and that here on earth we are only friends for a short time.

> May your heart open!
> May your heart draw near!
> You bring me torment,
> you bring me death.
> I will have to go there
> where I must perish.
> Will you weep for me one last time?
> Will you feel sad for me?
>
> Really we are only friends,
> I will have to go,
> I will have to go.[10]

The thought of the second poem is also pessimistic. It is the agonizing

[10] *Ibid.*, fol. 26 r.

84

question about the possibility of existence after death. "Is it true perhaps that one lives there, where we all go? Does your heart believe this?" Then when the poet thinks about the symbolism of flowers and songs, he inquires whether we can hope to be given, or even to be loaned there, a few songs, a few beautiful words. One thing is certain: "I will have to go down there," because God, the Giver of life, is also, paradoxically, "He who shrouds people in the grave."

> Given over to sadness
> we remain here on earth.
> Where is the road
> that leads to the Region of the Dead,
> the place of our downfall,
> the country of the fleshless?
>
> Is it true perhaps that one lives
> there, where we all go?
> Does your heart believe this?
> He hides us
> in a chest, in a coffer,
> the Giver of Life,
> He who shrouds people in the grave.
>
> Will I be able to look upon,
> able to see perhaps, the face
> of my mother, of my father?
> Will they loan me
> a few songs, a few words?
> I will have to go down there;
> nothing do I expect.
> They leave us,
> given over to sadness.[11]

The third poem seems to contradict the pessimism of the first two and shows that sadness was not universal in ancient Mexico. The author of this poem was able to look upon death with hope. Realizing that the earth is not a place of perfect happiness, he declares that pleasure does exist in the beyond, because otherwise we must believe that "only in vain have

[11] *Ibid.*, fol. 14 r.

85

we come to the earth." For him this would be unacceptable, because man is always fascinated by happiness. The forger of songs has surmounted the difficult step of death and believes that at last he will enjoy "the genuine flowers that bring happiness, that bring peace to the heart. . . ."

Truly I say:
certainly it is not the place of happiness
here on earth.
Certainly one must look somewhere else,
where indeed happiness will exist.
Or only in vain have we come to the earth?

Somewhere else is the place of life.
There I want to go,
there surely I will sing
with the most beautiful birds.
There I will have
genuine flowers,
the flowers that delight,
that bring peace to the heart,
the only ones that give peace to man,
that intoxicate him with joy. . . .[12]

These three poems show with a depth of poetic feeling what the wise men of ancient Mexico thought about love, hope, fear, and the supreme mystery of death.

The theme of war appears often in Náhuatl lyric poetry, linked with death, the glory of the gods, and the greatness of the people of the Sun. Songs proclaiming the glory and power of the Aztecs frequently reach an almost mystical exaltation. The following song speaks for itself:

From where the eagles are resting,
from where the tigers are exalted,
the Sun is invoked.

Like a shield that descends,
so does the Sun set.
In Mexico night is falling,
war rages on all sides.

[12] *Ibid.*, fol. 1 v.

86

Oh Giver of Life!
war comes near....

Proud of itself
is the city of Mexico-Tenochtitlan.
Here no one fears to die in war.
This is our glory.
This is Your Command,
oh Giver of Life!
Have this in mind, oh princes,
do not forget it.
Who could conquer Tenochtitlan?
Who could shake the foundation of heaven?

With our arrows,
with our shields,
the city exists.
Mexico-Tenochtitlan remains.[13]

While in Mexico-Tenochtitlan the greatness and power of the people of the Sun were often proclaimed, in other regions of the Náhuatl world, such as Huexotzinco, poets also composed songs in praise of the flowery wars which were waged for the purpose of obtaining prisoners, and they also exhorted their warriors not to fear death in the struggle. The following poem is a brilliant description of a battle in one of the flowery wars:

There is a clamor of bells,
the dust rises as if it were smoke.
The Giver of Life is gratified.
Shield flowers open their blossoms,
the glory spreads,
it becomes linked to earth.
Death is here among the flowers
in the midst of the plain!
Close to the war,
when the war begins,
in the midst of the plain,
the dust rises as if it were smoke,

13 *Ibid.*, fol. 19 v.–20 r.

entangled and twisted round
with flowery strands of death.
Oh Chichimec princes!
Do not fear, my heart!
In the midst of the plain
my heart craves death
by the obsidian edge.
Only this my heart craves:
death in war....[14]

There are many other poems about war. Those translated above show that the Nahuas had a deep lyrical feeling for what they considered their supreme mission: to dominate the peoples of the four corners of the universe and make them vassals of the Giver of Life.

A great deal of time could be spent studying the purely lyric poetry of the Nahuas. In addition to those already presented, there are other compositions in which Náhuatl wise men expressed what can be called their philosophical thought, their doubts, and their inquiry. A poem which sources attribute to the famous king Nezahualcóyotl poses the problem of finding satisfaction in earthly things:

What have you been seeking?
Where has your heart been wandering?
Giving your heart to each little thing,
you leave it without direction;
you lose your heart.
Can something be found on earth?[15]

In another poem the same author gave an answer in the language of symbolism. He had discovered the meaning of flower-and-song which he expressed in four clear lines:

At last my heart knows;
for now I hear a song,
I contemplate a flower
which will not wither![16]

[14] *Ibid.*, fol. 9 r.
[15] *Ibid.*, fol. 2 v.
[16] MSS *Romances de los Señores de la Nueva España*, fol. 19 v.

Nezahualcóyotl sought in his heart songs and flowers that would endure forever. Aware of death, he hoped that at least these might be carried to the innermost house of the Lord of the Close and Near, where dwell the birds with golden feathers:

> They shall not wither, my flowers,
> they shall not cease, my songs.
> I, the singer, lift them up.
> They are scattered, they spread about.
> Even though on earth my flowers
> may wither and yellow,
> they will be carried there,
> to the innermost house
> of the bird with the golden feathers.[17]

Like several other Náhuatl wise men and poets, Nezahualcóyotl succeeded in expressing himself by means of flower-and-song. The part of his work that has come down to us gives his ideas and sentiments about man's existence on earth, about death and the beyond, and about the mysteries that surround the supreme Giver of Life, the Lord of the Close and Near. Many rewarding discoveries await whoever explores in depth this form of more personal lyric poetry among the Nahuas.

From the world of the Mayas there are some extant lyric compositions in various books of *Chilam Balam* among mythical and semi-historical texts. Among these are the prophecies which at times seem to resemble the words of ancient Hebrew prophets. An example of this form of lyric poetry is the poem attributed to a singer and prophet in ancient Maní, some years before the arrival of the Spanish conquerors. It is an extremely beautiful and majestic poem with an incisive force which doubtless was very impressive for those who heard it from the prophet's own lips.

> On the day 13-Ahau,
> the *katún* [twenty-year period] will come to an end,
> in the time of the Itzá,
> in the time of Tancah, Lord of Mayapán.
> There is the sign of the one and only God.

[17] *Cantares Mexicanos*, fol. 16 v.

The sacred tree will come,
it shall be manifest to all,
so that the world shall be enlightened, oh father.
It will be the beginning of strife,
the beginning of rivalry,
the man-priest will come,
he will bring the sign of God
in time to come, oh father!
Shouting from a distance,
he will come and you will see the pheasant
which flies over the tree of life.
A new day shall dawn in the north,
it will dawn in the west,
Itzam will disappear.
Our father comes very close, oh Itzá!
Your elder brother is coming,
he who is before the sacred stone.
Receive your guests,
the bearded men,
the men who come from the east,
the bearers of the sign of God.
Good and wise is the word
of God which comes to us.
Comes the day of our life,
do not lose it in the world, oh father. . . .
It is the beginning of the men
of the second term.
Let us raise on high the sign,
let us raise up the tree of life.
Everything will change in a moment.
The successor will appear,
of the first tree on earth.
The change will be manifest to all.
From the sky he comes,
he who spreads the word,
for you,
to give you life. Oh Itzá!
It will dawn for those who believe,

within the next *katún*, oh father!
Believe in these my words,
I, the Chilam Balam,
I have explained to the world the word of God,
so that it be heard
to the limits of this earth, oh father!
It is the word of God,
Lord of heaven and earth.
Good indeed is his word in the heavens, oh father![18]

The preceding poem, a kind of prophecy about the coming of the conquistadors and Christians, is in sharp contrast to the following lyric song in which the Mayas bewailed the results of the Conquest:

The foreigners made it different
when they arrived here.
They brought shameful things
when they came here. . . .
No fortunate days
were granted to us then. . . .
This was the cause of our sickness.
No more fortunate days for us
no more just decisions.
And in the end we lost our vision,
it was our shame.
Everything shall be revealed![19]

Prophecies and predictions about the *katúns* and chronicles and lyric accounts of the Spanish Conquest, together with other songs, are found in the various Yucatec books of *Chilam Balam*. There are several publications which give extracts from this kind of lyric and prophetic works translated into English. Especially recommended is the edition of *The Book of Chilam Balam of Chumayel* by Ralph L. Roys, which includes the entire Maya text with an English version.

Of a different flavor are many of the poems, sacred hymns, and more personal lyric compositions in the already mentioned *The Book of the*

18 Roys, *Chilam Balam of Chumayel*, 167–68. *Maya text*, 106.

19 *Ibid.*, 83. Maya text, 22.

Songs of Dzitbalché. An example of the latter is the following song, a declaration of the joy which can be found everywhere on earth:

You are singing, little dove,
on the branches of the silk-cotton tree.
And there also is the cuckoo,
and many other little birds.
All are rejoicing,
the songbirds of our god, our Lord.
And our goddess
has her little birds,
the turtledove, the redbird,
the black and yellow songbirds, and the hummingbird.
These are the birds of the beautiful goddess, our Lady.
If there is such happiness
among the creatures,
why do our hearts not also rejoice?
At daybreak all is jubilant.
Let only joy, only songs,
enter our thoughts![20]

There are also a number of lyric compositions scattered through the *Popol Vuh* of the Quiché Mayas of Guatemala. One example is the *camucú* or song of farewell chanted by four Quiché elders, expressing the sadness in their hearts when they must leave their people. As in the case of Náhuatl poetry, this translation attempts to preserve the style of the native language and especially the parallel phrases:

Oh our children!
We go away
but we will return.
We leave you wise counsel;
and to you also,
healthy advice,
oh our women,
who have come from a distant land.
We return to our home.
Our Lord of the Deer is there in His place,

[20] *El Libro de los Cantares de Dzitbalché,* 80.

He is manifest in the heavens.
We begin the return,
having completed our mission,
our days being fulfilled.
Think of us,
do not erase us from memory,
do not forget us;
continue to see your homes
and your mountains.
Be firmly established there.
Thus may it be!
Continue on your way
and you will see again
the place from which we all come.[21]

These examples of lyric Maya poetry show the variety of subjects it covered. Truly, much of the soul of this cultured people is reflected in the later texts, expressions of their thought and sentiment.

The not very well-known Otomí people, who have lived for hundreds of years on Mexico's central plateau, are noted for their deep artistic sensitiveness, although theirs was not one of the great cultures such as the Maya and Náhuatl. The Otomís were oppressed most of the time. While some of their lords managed to remain relatively independent, the greater part of this people was conquered by one state after another throughout the centuries of pre-Hispanic history.

But if the Otomís were often scorned by those who ruled them, at least they had the unusual privilege of watching the birth, the rise, and the fall of many native "empires." Probably they witnessed the ruin of Teotihuacán; surely they saw the collapse of Tula, the Toltec metropolis; and finally, with the advent of the Spaniards, the end of Mexico-Tenochtitlan.

The Otomís, accustomed to being looked down upon, accepted their plight without bitterness, with an immutable smile. They also left a few testimonies of how they felt and reacted. The following are some examples

[21] *Popol Vuh: The Sacred Book of the Ancient Quiché Maya*, 204–205; Quiché text, *Popol Vuh: Das Heilige Buch der Quiché-Indianer von Guatemala*, 142.

of their ancient lyric poetry, which was preserved in translation in the manuscript *Cantares Mexicanos*. One song, described in the text as a "song of Otomí sadness," conveys something of their depth of feeling.

When I suffer,
I make myself strong within.
If we are sad,
if we go weeping through the world,
truly, in a single moment it will finish.[22]

The same theme often expressed in various Náhuatl compositions—the theme of the poet who seeks flowers, quetzal feathers, and jades in order to express what he feels—appears again in the following Otomí song from the same manuscript in the National Library:

I polish jades,
sparkling in the sun.
On the paper I am putting
feathers of the green and black bird.
I know the origin of songs:
I only arrange the gold-colored feathers.
It is a beautiful song!
I, the singer, weave precious jades,
show how the blossoms open.
With this I please
the Lord of the Close and Near.[23]

In addition to these examples of Otomí poetry, several contemporary researchers have gathered compositions which also appear to be ancient. The deep lyric sentiment of the Otomí soul shines in the simple beauty of the following verse in which one imagines a young girl speaking:

Little flower, little flower,
I am flowering too.
Pluck me, pluck me, whoever may wish.
By myself, I will not move.[24]

[22] *Cantares Mexicanos*, fol. 5 r.

[23] *Ibid.*, fol. 3 r.

[24] Jacques Soustelle, *La Famille Otomí-Pame du Mexique Central*, 250.

And illustrated here are Otomí words in praise of a woman loved:

In the sky, a moon;
on your face, a mouth.
In the sky, many stars;
on your face, only two eyes.[25]

This final verse is a simple expression of Otomí thought about the meaning of life:

The river passes, passes,
never stops.
The wind passes, passes,
never stops.
Life passes,
never returns.[26]

These examples of Otomí verse show the subjects they used as well as their individual style. Here also are metaphors and parallelisms similar to those found in the Náhuatl, Maya, and other native poetry. Although this is a lesser voice, it still confirms the existence of a rich lyric poetry in the early days of indigenous Mexico.

It only remains to add that verse still survives among the descendants of many of these groups. Anyone visiting native communities will discover this for himself. A study of the contemporary poetry of Mexican natives would uncover some truly extraordinary present-day compositions not only by the Nahuas, Mayas, and Otomís, but also by such groups as the Tarascans, Zapotecs, Mixtecs, Huichols, Tarahumaras, and some others. But this discussion must be limited to a few examples from the rich legacy of the main pre-Columbian cultures of Mexico.

[25] Garibay K., *Historia de la Literatura Náhuatl*, I, 239.
[26] *Ibid.*, 238–39.

IV

Religious Celebrations and Drama

PUBLIC PERFORMANCES in pre-Columbian Mexico, as in other ancient cultures, had a religious origin. Sacred and ritualistic celebrations and festivals were the occasion for the beginning of drama. Evidence of this is given by murals discovered in Teotihuacán and by bas-reliefs at several Maya sites which show processions of priests and lords dressed to represent the gods and chanting sacred hymns (indicated by the flowery volutes coming from their mouths). These processions and the ancient rites in which priests and initiates took the parts of gods, bringing the divine songs to the people, mark the start of what later became drama. From other native cultures, such as the Tarascans of Michoacán, there are clay figurines of people wearing a variety of costumes acting and performing different dances. It is even possible that some of the figurines remaining from the Pre-Classic Period before the Christian era also represent singers and dancers dressed for the festivals.

Besides these testimonies discovered by archaeological research, there are ancient accounts which frequently mention dances and hymns sung on special occasions, always concerning the cult of the gods. For example, after a battle was won, thanks were given for the victory with dances and songs to the appropriate deity. Similar performances, with their corresponding rites and invocations, took place to install an important lord, to ask for abundant rain and good crops, or to evoke intervention by the gods.

With the passing of time, the sequence of hymns and the order of the dances and actions performed became firmly established. When the conquistadors arrived, they found in ancient Mexico fixed customs regulating the ceremonial plays, dances, hymns, and dialogues, which together with the sacrifices were the focus of attention in the many religious fiestas. Fray Diego de Durán described how the Nahuas arranged and acted out sacred plays during their festivals.

> Those Indians had many ways of dancing and merrymaking to celebrate the religion fiestas of their gods, composing different songs to each idol according to his importance and greatness. And thus many days before the feast days came, there were long rehearsals of songs and dances for that day; and with each new song they brought out different costumes and ornaments, with mantles and feathers and false hair and masks, according to the songs they had composed and what they were about; and according to the ceremony and the festival, they dressed themselves sometimes as eagles and lions or as soldiers, Huaxtec Indians, hunters, monkeys, or dogs, and a thousand other disguises.[1]

As Durán's words indicate, the songs, dances, and acting which took place during the festivals were well known in advance. The use of costumes and masks already indicates the theatrical nature of these ceremonies.

A study of the various festivals and sacrifices in which the Náhuatl-speaking people honored their gods reveals that there was a perpetual cycle of religious drama which unfolded through their year composed of eighteen months of twenty days each. This form of perpetual and sacred theater actually had a double nature. On the one hand were the priests, the students in the *calmécac* and *telpochcalli*, and the people in general who took part in the festivities and plays, sometimes wearing disguises and being present during the dialogue with the gods. All of them chanted hymns and went through a set form of action, which dramatized the symbolism of the religious doctrines and the ancient myths. But along with this action in which all participated, there was something else which is revolting to our way of thinking: the special "actors" who impersonated, in an almost mystical way, the deities themselves. These actors played their parts only once, for their destiny was to be united by means of sacrifice with the gods they represented. There are descriptions of how

[1] *Historia de las Indias de Nueva España y Islas de Tierra Firme*, II, 231.

those who were to act out the roles of gods and end their lives in sacrifice learned their roles.

Usually for several days before each festival the dances and songs were taught and rehearsed in the late afternoon, either in the main plaza or in front of the temple of the divinity whose feast day was approaching. On the day of the feast and sometimes during the preceding night, the songs began with music of flutes, drums, and bells. About the same time the one who was to represent the god came out dressed in his costume and danced the dance of that particular ceremony or *netotiliztli*. Sometimes all the people danced, including students of the *calmécac* and *telpochcalli*, young girls, and even occasionally the *ahuianime* or public women. Some disguised themselves as wild animals, eagles, serpents, or as different kinds of birds. For instance, on the feast of Atamalqualiztli there were unusual costumes, among others, those called "masks of sleep."

The priests and choirs of young girls and students also took part in the singing. There were dialogues between different choirs, solemnly recalling myths and religious beliefs. Often a priest spoke in the name of the people or in the name of the one who was to give his life. At the end came the sacrifices, a ritualistic act of the most profound dramatic significance, in which quail and other birds were offered and, as a climax, one or more human victims. Sometimes there was a symbolic struggle on the *temalácatl* or stone where the captive, with unequal arms and one foot hobbled, confronted a well-armed warrior who came up to fight him. Sometimes a young girl or young man, representing the goddess or the god, went up to the sacrificial stone so that their heart might be offered, in this way contributing with their blood to the maintenance of the life of the Sun. Actually, most of the victims who represented a god learned their parts perfectly, as was the case of the young boy who personified Tezcatlipoca in the Tóxcatl fiesta. He symbolically broke a flute as he bade farewell to the pleasures of the world, climbing the steps of the temple where he was to die. And the young girls who represented Xilonen, the goddess of tender maize, or Xochiquetzalli or Tlazoltéotl and other divinities also played their parts. They were all trained to act just once in the cosmic drama of the Aztec perpetual theater. They were messengers from the people, collaborators with the Sun, carefully chosen to begin their journey to the beyond.

The following description, taken from the calendar's repertoire of festivals, tells about the annual ceremony in honor of Tláloc, the rain god, whose feast day corresponded to the twenty-ninth of April on our calendar. According to Father Durán:

> The feast of this god took place on the twenty-ninth of April and was so solemn and important that every king and lord, the old and the young, all came with their offerings from every part of the land. Indeed, the celebration of this idol fell in the month which their calendar called Huey Tozoztli. It was solemn and important, with double ceremonies and rites, because it coincided with one of the festivals which they had every twenty days. . . . It was devoted to petitioning a good year for the maize which was already sprouting.[2]

The festival was celebrated at the same time in different places, of which two were most important: the mountain of Tláloc or Tlalocan south of Tezcoco and in front of the main temple in Tenochtitlan which was consecrated to Huitzilopochtli and Tláloc. The lords of Mexico, Tezcoco, and Tlacopan, as well as a great many people, went in procession to the mountain of Tláloc, on the slopes of which huts of branches had been built. On the top was the sanctuary where the ceremony was celebrated.

Meanwhile, in Tenochtitlan almost the entire population participated in the celebration which took place in front of the main temple. Before the ceremony they arranged an artificial woods with trees, which was a kind of stage. In the middle of some bushes and shrubs was a very tall tree surrounded by four others oriented towards the four points of the compass. Round about flew banners spattered with melted rubber, a symbolic decoration in honor of Tláloc. When the moment for the ceremony came, as Durán writes:

> The priests and dignitaries, all very adorned, took out a little girl of seven or eight years who was in a kind of tent, completely covered over, where no one had seen her, where the lords had hidden the child. In this manner

2 *Ibid.*, 117.

the priests took out on their shoulders the child who had been put in that tent, all dressed in blue, which represented the great lake and all the fountains and small rivers, with a band of reddish leather around her head and fastened to it a tuft of blue feathers. They placed this little girl who was in that tent in the woods, under that tall tree, facing towards the idol, and then they brought a drum and all sat down without dancing, with the girl in front, and they sang many and varied songs.[3]

One of the songs chanted in the festival of Tláloc has survived, thanks to Sahagún's informants. In the form of a dialogue, it asks the rain god for abundant showers. A choir, probably made up of young students of the *calmécac*, begins the song stating the meaning and purpose of the festival: they have come to beg Tláloc to send heavy rains so that the maize will grow and men will live. They beg Tláloc to loan the rain, for they expect to pay for his gift. The sacrifices are the manner in which they will repay the debt they will contract.

Choir:
> In Mexico we beg a loan from the god.
> There are the banners of paper
> and at the four corners
> men are standing.

The verse is repeated, probably by the people, and then the priest himself addresses the divinity, imploring rain. The priest of Tláloc mentions the victims to be offered in the festival. They are small children whose weeping, when they are sacrificed, will be an omen of heavy rain. These children, whose crying is awaited are symbolically referred to as bundles of blood-stained ears of corn.

Priest of Tláloc:
> Now it is time for you to weep!
> Alas, I was created
> and for my god
> festal bundles of blood-stained ears of corn
> I carry now
> to the divine hearth.

[3] *Ibid.*, 141–42.

You are my chief, Prince and Magician,
and though in truth
it is you who produces our sustenance,
although you are the first,
we only cause you shame.

Again the choir of students or perhaps another group of priests replies in the name of Tláloc. The god exhorts the people and the priesthood to venerate him and recognize his power:

Tláloc:
If anyone
has caused me shame,
it is because he did not know me well;
you are my fathers, my priesthood,
Serpents and Tigers.

Then the priest of the rain god begins to chant another song, mentioning the mansion of Tlalocan and asking the god to spread out over all parts to make the beneficent rain fall.

Priest of Tláloc:
In Tlalocan, in the turquoise vessel,
it is wont to come forth, but now is not seen
Acatónal.
Spread out in Poyauhtlan,
in the region of mist!
With timbrels of mist
our word is carried to Tlalocan....

The choir, now speaking in the name of the victim, the little girl dressed in blue who will be sacrificed to the rain god, chants several verses of deep religious significance. The victim will go away forever. She will be sent to the Place of Mystery. Now is the time for her crying. But perhaps in four year's time there will be a transformation, a rebirth, there in the region-of-the-fleshless. He who propagates men may send once more to this earth some of the children who were sacrificed. In veiled form this hints at a kind of reincarnation, which is very seldom mentioned in the ancient texts. Now the choir speaks once more for the child:

Choir [speaking in the name of the victim]:
I will go away forever,
it is time for crying.
Send me to the Place of Mystery,
under your command.
I have already told
the Prince of the Sad Omen,
I will go away forever,
it is time for crying.
In four years
comes the arising among us,
many people
without knowing it;
in the place of the fleshless,
the house of quetzal feathers,
is the transformation.
It is the act of the Propagator of Men.

—Death

The priest of Tláloc repeats the invocation to the god of rain. He begs him once more to be present in all parts, to make fertile the land sown with seed, to spread out and make the rain fall.

Priest of Tláloc:
Go to all parts,
spread out
in Poyauhtlan,
in the region of mist.
With timbrels of mist
our word is carried to Tlalocan.[4]

After this hymn was finished, the dances continued without interruption, with the priests and people probably chanting other songs in honor of the rain god, until the lords and priests who had gone to the mountain of Tláloc returned to perform the concluding rites of the festival. According to the testimony of Durán and Sahagún's informants, they then went out on the lake in richly decorated canoes to where the water whirled round. There they cast down the large tree which had been set up in

---

[4] Garibay K., *Veinte Himnos Sacros de los Nahuas*, 51–52.

front of the main temple, and the little girl was sacrificed. They let her blood fall into the water, and also threw in a great number of jewels and ornaments which immediately disappeared in the whirlpool. Those who had officiated then went back to the city, and the ceremony was finished. The ritualistic drama, beseeching rain with the dances and songs of deep significance, had been acted out.

Descriptions such as this could be given for the other festivals in the so-called perpetual theater which prevailed in the pre-Hispanic Náhuatl world.

The Maya groups developed other forms of acting in addition to religious festivals and celebrations very similar to those of the Nahuas. The chroniclers of Yucatán, particularly Diego de Landa and López de Cogolludo, mention the existence of plays among the pre-Hispanic Mayas. Unfortunately most of the earlier plays vanished with the coming of the Conquest. In their place was born a new form of drama which, while retaining native elements such as the dances and songs, had very different plots and objectives as a result of the recently introduced Christian faith. There also appeared "pastorelas" or Christmas performances and allegorical plays with religious themes, as well as dramatic representations recalling the Spanish Conquest. Sometimes the works of Spanish authors were translated and adapted to indigenous languages; this was the case with *El gran teatro del mundo*, an allegorical poem by Calderón de la Barca, which was translated into Náhuatl.[5]

From the Quiché Mayas of Guatemala at least one piece has been found which seems to be almost entirely pre-Hispanic. It is the *Rabinal Achí*, preserved in the Quiché tongue. As previously mentioned, it was written down by the *abbé* Brasseur de Bourbourg from the text in the possession of the native elder Bartolo Ziz, who knew it as tradition and had it in recorded form about the middle of the nineteenth century. Brasseur himself saw a performance of *Rabinal Achí* on the twenty-fifth of January, 1856, in the village of Rabinal, now in the department of Baja Verapaz in Guatemala.

---

[5] See William A. Hunter, "The Calderonian Auto Sacramental 'El Gran Teatro del Mundo,' An edition and translation of a Náhuatl version," in *The Native Theatre in Middle America*.

The plot of the drama is the capture of a lord of the Quichés, the Quiché Man, with long dialogues between him and Rabinal Achí, and finally the death of the captive. The main characters are the prisoner himself and Rabinal Achí, son of the chief Hobtoh who determines the fate of the Quiché prisoner. There is also Ixoc-Mun, principal servant of the Rabinal lord, and some slaves and vassals who speak a few words. The rest of the characters have no speaking parts. Among them are the princess, "Mother of the small green birds," who is to dance with the prisoner, and a number of men and women slaves, eagle and tiger knights, and people of the village of Rabinal.

The play opens with long speeches by the Quiché Man and Rabinal Achí. The dialogue, which proceeds at great length, tells of the deeds and valor of the prisoner and the reasons why he has fought. A group of dancers weave round about the two speakers. Rabinal Achí finally catches the Quiché Man with a lasso and ties him to a tree from where he must listen to the heroic deeds of the people of Rabinal. The music and the dance continue monotonously. Rabinal Achí reminds the prisoner of the harm he has caused his people. The Quiché Man tries to regain this freedom. Rabinal Achí informs his father Hobtoh about what has happened. His father replies that he will receive the Quiché Man only when he offers himself as a vassal. The Quiché Man is now free of his bindings, but instead of going to offer himself as vassal to Hobtoh, he tries to attack Rabinal Achí. Ixoc-Mun, the servant, intervenes to protect his master.

The Quiché Man, speaking to Hobtoh, makes it clear that he is prepared to accept death, but asks that he be granted the honors and privileges due his rank as a lord. He recounts once more his deeds. He prefers to be sacrificed rather than humble himself. They offer him food and drink, which he only tastes. According to custom, they allow him to dance with the young girl, "Mother of the small green birds," and also with the eagle and tiger knights. Then he is permitted to go to say farewell to his valleys and mountains.

The end of the play shows the return of the Quiché Man, who regrets that he has not been able to change himself into a squirrel or a bird and die up on the branch of a tree, looking at the mountains and the valleys of the land where he was born. The eagle and tiger knights surround the

Quiché lord, the dance continues, and one imagines that the sacrifice is taking place.

Both the subject and the action show a pre-Hispanic origin. This is confirmed by the long dialogues with their many polite native phrases, parallel expressions, and pre-Columbian metaphors and symbols. Beyond a doubt the *Rabinal Achí* is one of the most authentic examples of indigenous drama prior to the Conquest. The dramatic quality of this Quiché work is shown in the final dialogue in which the Quiché Man asks permission to bid farewell to his valleys and mountains. The words he says upon his return show that there was no lack of poetic feeling in this form of drama:

Quiché Man:

Chief Hobtoh, give me your permission, before the heavens, before the earth. This my voice says to your ears, to your face: grant me thirteen times twenty days, thirteen times twenty nights, so that I may go to say farewell to the face of my mountains, to the face of my valleys, where formerly I was wont to go to the four corners, to the four sides, searching for, finding, that necessary to nourish myself, to eat.

(No one replies to the Quiché Man, who disappears for a few moments, dancing. Then, without returning to the platform on which the chief Hobtoh is seated, he approaches the eagles and jaguars gathered in the middle of the court around something similar to an altar.)

Oh eagles! Oh jaguars! You said: "He went away." I did not go away; I only went to say farewell to the face of my mountains, to the face of my valleys, where I was wont to search for something to nourish myself, to eat, in the four corners, on the four sides.

Alas, oh heavens! Alas, oh earth! My resolution, my courage have been of no avail. I sought my way beneath the heavens, I sought my way on the earth, snatching the green stuff, snatching the caltrops and thorns. My resolution, my courage has profited nothing.

Alas, oh heavens! Alas, oh earth! Truly, must I die, perish here, under the heavens, on the earth?

Oh my gold! Oh my silver! Oh offspring of my arrow, offspring of my shield! Let my native stick, my native weapons, my garlands, my sandals, go to my mountains, to my valleys!

Take word of me to my governor, to my chieftain, because the voice of my governor, of my chieftain, said that for a long time my resolution, my courage, searches for, finds, my nourishment, my food.

Thus said the voice of my governor, my chieftain; but now he may not say this, since I await only my death, my destruction, under the heavens, on the earth.

Alas, oh heavens! Alas, oh earth! Now that I must die, I must perish, here under the heavens, on the earth, why can I not change myself into a squirrel, a bird, that dies on the branch of a tree, on the sprout of a tree, where it found its nourishment, what it ate, under the heavens, on the earth!

Oh eagles! Oh jaguars! Come then to fulfill your mission, to fulfill your duty; may your teeth, may your claws, kill me in an instant, for I am reaching out to my mountains, my valleys.

May the heavens, the earth, be with us all! Oh eagles! Oh tigers![6]

Plays like the *Rabinal Achí* were frequent among both the Mayas and Nahuas. From the latter there is even more information which allows something to be said about what might be called their farces and comedies. Fray Diego de Durán, writing about the Náhuatl schools for dance, made a clear distinction between the plays presented in festivals to honor the gods and others which he specifically called "farces, interludes, and songs of much mirth." Among other things, he wrote:

There is another dance of old men disguised as hunchbacks, which is very amusing and gay and produces much laughter. They also have a song and dance with jugglers in which they bring in a dunce who mixes up the words and pretends to understand backwards his master's orders. During this dance they bounce a huge pole with their feet with such dexterity that one marvels at the turns and twists they do. Some people thought this was the work of the devil, but on due consideration it is nothing more than a juggling with the feet, similar to juggling with the hands in Spain.

When I was a boy, I saw with my own eyes a school for this game in the district of San Pablo; there was an Indian very skilled in the art, and many young Indians from different provinces were taught there. . . .

6 *Rabinal Achí, Teatro Indígena Prehispánico*, 88–91.

Also they dance hanging from a high pole, up in the air, sometimes dressed like birds and sometimes like monkeys; they fly round in the air, letting themselves down by means of ropes which are fastened to a frame at the top of this pole and unwind little by little.

Other times they have dances in which they paint themselves, sometimes black, sometimes white, sometimes green, with feathers on their heads and feet. Here some women take part also. Men and women pretend to be drunk, carrying cups and pitchers in their hands, as if they were drinking; all this pretending gives great pleasure and relaxation to the people of the city; they are delighted by a thousand different kinds of games invented by those in the schools for dances and by farces and interludes and songs of much mirth.[7]

One of these farces is preserved in the *Colección de Cantares* at the National Library. In this farce, a kind of buffoon arrives in the Tlatelolco market plaza, in the northern section of the city of Mexico-Tenochtitlan. He acts in different costumes, rapidly and skilfully putting on different masks. First he is a human being, then a deer, a rabbit, a thrush with a red breast, a quetzal bird, a parrot, and finally the same funny man again. What he says is amusing, but it also contains something to think about. The people watch and are entertained by the buffoon, who says:

My fine master, I have come; I am here to laugh.
I'm a rascal. My singing is a flower;
it gets mixed up, then it gets untangled.
Oh, I'm a master in the house.

Now let us begin. Already there has come
the sweet-smelling flower; may it please you.
It is going to rain flowers;
may they please you!

I am scattering many different flowers.
I come to offer songs, intoxicating flowers.
Oh, I'm a rascal, who comes from there,
where the water flows.
I come to offer songs, intoxicating flowers.

Next, using a rabbit's head, he appears as a god of *pulque* (a native

7 Durán, *op. cit.*, 231–32.

wine) and again mentions the flowers and songs. Always acting like the animal he represents, he dances in front of the people.

> I who come am the Deer-Two-Rabbit,
> the Rabbit which bleeds,
> the Deer with big horns. . . .
> My fine master, my friends, we open
> his book of flowers, his book of songs.
> Whose?
> His.
> Erect is the Flowery Tree,
> it has many branches,
> it has grown large; now it is scattering flowers.
> We have come to listen at your threshold,
> on the branches you are walking, Precious Pheasant.
> You are singing. . . .

The buffoon then changes his costume and becomes a thrush with a red breast. He dances and sings, telling of poetry, laughter, and suffering:

> I'm a rascal.
> I am the thrush with a red breast,
> now I shrill my song: jojojojon.
>
> I come to make paintings
> where the courtyard spreads out;
> I am the thrush with a red breast;
> shrill, shrill, my song: jojojojon.
>
> I wink my eyes,
> as I go laughing;
> from within the court I come,
> into a flower I am changing myself,
> I am the Rabbit who suffers. . . .

Finally he becomes a chattering parrot, a wise parrot from the interior of Tula, who invites everyone to listen to his song. While speaking the last lines, the buffoon takes off his mask and sings an exquisite song in honor of poetry.

I am the chattering Parrot,
I go to catch it, I throw it. . . .
Now I begin, now I can sing.
From there I come, from the interior of Tula;
now can I sing; my voice bursts forth,
the flower has opened.
Listen to my song:
"Stealer of songs, oh my heart,
where can you find them?
You are in need. But like a painting
grasp firmly the black and red ink,
then perhaps you will no longer be a beggar."[8]

The people were delighted with this kind of entertainment, and when it was finished, they recompensed the buffoon. Few farces of this kind have survived, but these few give an idea of a style of acting which was very popular in the Náhuatl world.

The ancient texts at the same time also mention the so-called *tlaquetz-que*, "those who made things stand out," entertainers who roamed the plazas and market places of cities and villages, reciting the old poems and legends. The people crowded about them and enjoyed listening. Later on, in addition to "those who made things stand out," actors who acted out the legends and myths began to make their appearance. Their purpose was not to perform a ritual or sacrifice but rather to keep alive what everyone knew by tradition.

In the *mise en scène* of the famous myth concerning the flight of the culture hero Quetzalcóatl, he leaves Tula to go towards the east, to Tlilan, Tlapalan, the place of the black and red color, the land of wisdom. When this text is read even today, the action which accompanied it can be imagined. Probably a singer started the poem, which tells of the departure of Quetzalcóatl, "our prince," Nácxitl Topiltzin, from Tula:

There was in Tula a house with crossbeams of wood.
Today remain only the columns of serpent form;
he left them, Nácxitl Topiltzin, when he went away.

---

[8] A. M. Garibay K. (ed.), *"Poema de Travesuras," Cantares Mexicanos*, fol. 67 r. Published in *Tlalocan*, III, No. 2 (1952), 142–46.

A choir responds:

> To the sound of trumpets our people are mourning.
> Now he is going away, to disappear there in Tlapalan.

The first singer continues his story:

> We will go through Cholula,
> through the place of rains,
> close to Poyauhtécatl,
> the lord of mist,
> to the place where are the canoes.
> To the sound of trumpets our people are mourning.
> Now he is going away, to disappear there in Tlapalan.

At this point the actor representing Quetzalcóatl, "our prince," and his large retinue which is going to pass through Cholula, close to the mountain of mist, come out in their costumes and masks. Probably there also were various dance steps in which not only the actors but some of the people participated. Then two historical characters, Ihuiquecholli and Matlacxóchitl, appear. The latter is to be Quetzalcóatl's successor among the Toltecs. Both lament that the great lord has left them to go to Tlapalan:

Ihuiquecholli:
> From Nonoalco I come,
> I, the bird of fine feathers,
> I, the prince, Mamali,
> grieved am I.

Matlacxóchitl:
> My lord has gone,
> he of the fine feathers,
> he has left me fatherless,
> me, Matlacxóchitl.

Ihuiquecholli:
> The mountains are cleft,
> for this I weep,
> heaved up are the sands,
> for this I weep.

Matlacxóchitl:
> My lord has gone,
> he of the splendid feathers,
> he has left me fatherless,
> me, Matlacxóchitl.

Again the choir and the principal singer alternately describe the places through which Quetzalcóatl, accompanied by some of his attendants, is passing. Here are a few lines of their dialogue:

Singer:
> In the place of the mist he is no longer,
> in the place of the mist he is no longer.

Choir:
> How will all your courtyards remain forsaken?
> How will your palaces remain forsaken?
> Oh, you have left them orphans here in Tula, in Nonoalco!

Singer:
> Even you yourself are weeping, Prince Tímal.
> Even you yourself are weeping, Prince Tímal.

The actors dance once more. Quetzalcóatl and those who march with him go farther away as they continue their journey. At last they leave the plaza where the old myth is being acted out. Then comes the final dialogue between the principal singer and the choir:

Singer:
> In wood and in stone you remain engraved
> there in Tula; we are wailing.

Choir:
> Oh, Nácxitl, our prince,
> never will your glory be dimmed;
> for this your vassals will mourn.
> Only the house of jade remains standing,
> the house of serpents which you leave upright
> there in Tula; we are wailing.[9]

[9] *Cantares Mexicanos,* fol. 26 v.

Thus the Nahuas kept alive the great myths and legends through dances, costumes, hymns, and dialogues. And there is even some indication that while acting out the myths, they had already begun to interpret them in different ways, searching for deeper significance, as happened also in Greek theater. They attempted to give interpretations of the meaning of life, the problems which must be confronted and the happy or unhappy outcomes awaiting man. Unfortunately, only fragments remain, but these give us a hint about the change which was taking place.

The study of the native texts of pre-Hispanic Náhuatl theater still holds many surprises. For instance, there are fragments showing what appears to have been an attempt to emancipate the plays and performances from strictly religious themes in order to introduce into them problems of everyday life. In these appear warriors, women who dispense pleasure, fathers of families, merchants, and even the poor victims who are going to strictly religious themes in order to introduce into them problems of their suffering and problems and yearning to find at last "the flower-and-song of things."

In the often quoted *Cantares Mexicanos* there are a few fragments under the heading *xochicuícatl cuecuechtli,* which means, literally, "light poetry." The following few lines are from one of these which almost certainly was a part of this new style of play. It is called "Song of the Harlots." The characters are mostly women. Chalchiuhnene and Nanotzin are both *ahuianime* or "gladdeners," women of pleasure. The mother of Nanotzin appears, as well as Quetzalmiyahuaxóchitl and Quetzalxóchitl, two other *ahuianime* who are more or less reformed. There is also a young man, Ahuítzotl, who may represent the Aztec *tlatoani* of the same name or may be merely a namesake. Here is the dialogue between the first two "gladdeners," Chalchiuhnene and Nanotzin:

Chalchiuhnene:
Were you hurt, sister Nanotzin?

Nanotzin:
I don't know yet, Chalchiuhnene.
Let's go home. My mother is there.

Chalchiuhnene:
> He came alone ... you saw that ...
> a woman who already has a man ....
> I want to go home.

Nanotzin:
> Let's go home. My mother's there.

Chalchiuhnene:
> Nanotzin, where did that happen?

Nanotzin:
> I could die, my friend!
> Of course he doesn't even know.
> There's my mother.

The dialogue is certainly obscure. Apparently the two women are talking about a complication in the love life of Nanotzin. The two "gladdeners" go toward the house where they find Nanotzin's mother waiting for them. The mother brings them in and asks her daughter to stay with her so that she will be at peace.

The mother:
> Come in here with me,
> that way I will be at peace,
> and at peace I must be!

The other women, Quetzalmiyahuaxóchitl and Quetzalxóchitl, who have been called "reformed gladdeners," now appear. The first, speaking to Nanotzin's mother, expresses her disgust with life.

Quetzalmiyahuaxóchitl:
> I am sick at heart, my mother.
> Men are happy, those who live in pleasure,
> but perhaps you overlook it here.
> You scold me for that!
> My man lived in pleasure, my mother.
> Perhaps they saw me?
> Perhaps I didn't know?
> Alas, now I can cry,
> I, Quetzalmiyahuaxóchitl, the gladdener.

Some still come to me.
I will die this way.

Then she turns toward Nanotzin, about whose difficulties she has heard. She, too, has suffered but now she has learned to laugh at herself. As a friend she gives this advice:

Quetzalmiyahuaxóchitl:
I just laugh at myself!
Why? Are you like me, my friend?
I cried about it,
I said I would die. . . .
Now, I just laugh at myself!

Quetzalxóchitl, the other reformed gladdener, says she has scolded her friends who continue to live a dissolute life. It is better to love oneself than to go on giving oneself to others:

Quetzalxóchitl:
I am Quetzalxóchitl.
I love myself, I who am a fine woman.
I scold my friends,
Cozcamalintzin and Xiuhtlamiyahuatzin.
They live a dissolute life,
carefully washing their hair.
My mother, you, my mother,
scold my friends,
Cozcamalintzin and Xiuhtlamiyahuatzin.
They live a dissolute life,
carefully washing their hair.

At this point, in a kind of interlude, the young Ahuítzotl appears reciting a poem which expresses trivial ideas but also sad feelings. Evidently influenced by Ahuítzotl's thoughts, Nanotzin, the "gladdener," speaks once more. She is doubtful. Speaking of the pleasures, she feels that she is in danger of being cast aside like a withered flower.

Nanotzin:
What shall I do? My man compares me
to a wild red flower.

When I have withered in his hands,
he will leave me.[10]

This is only an example of the truly dramatic dialogue found in these texts described as "light poetry." As already mentioned, there are other equally interesting fragments still waiting to be studied. A thorough analysis of these will show how far pre-Hispanic theater went along this path. What was saved from oblivion, fragmentary as it is, still gives a glimpse of the richness and uniqueness of native American drama which had its beginnings in the sacred feasts and developed in isolation its own original forms of expression.

[10] *Ibid.*, fol. 75 v.

V

Chronicles and History

THE WISE MEN AND PRIESTS of ancient Mexico were masters in the art of measuring time. The Mayas, who had a calendar which was closer to the solar year than our own Gregorian calendar, have left in their steles and codices ample proof of their preoccupation with time. For them, to assign a date was to know, perhaps even to identify themselves with, the ever changing nature of the universe. Time was not an abstract concept; it was a living reality, a deity, the cosmic substratum of everything. Some of the Maya inscriptions on stone, commemorating events of importance, date from the beginnings of the Christian era.

Other pre-Hispanic high cultures, among whom the Aztecs were outstanding and also including the enigmatic Olmecs, the Zapotecs and Mixtecs, the inhabitants of Teotihuacán and Tula, and those who inherited from them, have handed down to posterity, in spite of the destruction by the Conquest, a number of calendric inscriptions and some historical texts. It is sufficient to recall that their notations on stone, on animal skins, and on the *amate* paper of their codices offer many examples of their ideographic and partially phonetic systems of writing. Linked with this was the constant and well-organized memorizing of legends, chronicles, and history in the pre-Hispanic schools. It is principally because of this, together with the archaeological discoveries, that something of the history of these peoples can be reconstructed.

An eloquent testimony is offered by the following text which, just as in the case of the Mayas, shows the concern of the Aztecs to preserve the memory of their past. These are the words set down by the historian Tezozómoc in the introduction to his *Crónica Mexicáyotl*:

Thus they have come to tell it,
thus they have come to record it in their narration,
and for us they have painted it in their codices,
the ancient men, the ancient women.
They were our grandfathers, our grandmothers,
our great-grandfathers, great-grandmothers,
our great-great-grandfathers, our ancestors.
Their account was repeated,
they left it to us;
they bequeathed it forever
to us who live now,
to us who come down from them.

Never will it be lost, never will it be forgotten,
that which they came to do,
that which they came to record in their paintings:
their renown, their history, their memory.
Thus in the future
never will it perish, never will it be forgotten,
always we will treasure it,
we, their children, their grandchildren,
brothers, great-grandchildren,
great-great-grandchildren, descendants,
we who carry their blood and their color,
we will tell it, we will pass it on
to those who do not yet live, who are to be born,
the children of the Mexicans, the children of the Tenochcans. . . .[1]

The interest ancient Mexicans had in their past is obvious. But what was their concept of history, what subjects did it cover, and what stylistic procedures were used in recording accounts of the past?

In Mexico, as in other ancient cultures, the first memories were handed down dressed in the guise of legend and myth. The long epic poems previously quoted tell in symbol and metaphor the beginnings of cosmic happenings, of gods and men. Later came compositions which recorded the deeds of heroes, their victories and their defeats.

But the entrance into history proper is marked by the commemorative

---

[1] Fernando Alvarado Tezozómoc, *Crónica Mexicáyotl*, 4–6.

inscriptions, the annals and chronicles in which were set down the most important events together with the dates assigned. Among these events are the long pilgrimages and the arrival at different places, the birth, election, and death of rulers, and the exact time when a war or some natural phenomenon such as the eruption of a volcano or some other catastrophe occurred. Some of the few remaining pre-Columbian codices are examples of this form of chronicle. There are a few extant Mixtec codices which also show how precisely were recorded the genealogy and descent of governors and nobles. Other manuscripts outlined the limits of public domains, the various distributions of land, amounts of tribute, the sequence to be followed in religious fiestas and ceremonies, and the attributes of the gods, not to mention the divinatory almanacs and many other items concerning cultural institutions. Obviously the aim of these kinds of records was to establish points of contact with the past, indicating by means of the calendar the dates of important happenings. But native history grew into something greater. Just as in the Near East, India, and China, what were at first simple chronicles and factual notations came to be enriched with more elaborate comments on the character of the persons mentioned, the causes of principal events, and even some aspects of daily life at that time.

Many of these additional commentaries were not recorded; they were memorized systematically in the schools where the content of the codices was taught. It is because of these commentaries, written down in the indigenous languages soon after the Conquest, that today we know more about the principal institutions which prevailed in the various cultures of ancient Mexico. Found in these commentaries are remarks on the character of some of the rulers and the reasons for wars. They also give a glimpse of the social, political, and religious organizations and show the importance of the commercial expeditions and the organization of the markets and the schools—in other words, the steady throb of their daily life. The best examples are the many texts, mainly chronicles, which have been preserved in the Náhuatl language and in the tongues of the Maya family and a few from other groups such as the Otomís and the Tarascans.

Additional evidence of the importance which ancient Mexicans attached to history is found in the fact that they even used it as an instrument for political control. In the *Códice Matritense*, written in Náhuatl, is recorded an account which tells that after the Aztecs had defeated Azcapotzalco and won their independence around 1427, King Itzcóatl ordered the ancient codices to be burned so that a new official version of Aztec history could be established. Realizing the value of tradition and conscious of the fact that up to that time the Aztecs were known only as a poor and persecuted people, Itzcóatl decided that new codices should be painted in which his nation would appear as the chosen people of the Sun, heirs of the Toltecs and future rulers of ancient Mexico. This is a translation of the text which speaks of this concern to implant a new historical consciousness:

Their history was preserved.
But then it was burned,
when Itzcóatl reigned in Mexico.
A decision was taken,
the Mexican lords said:
"It is not suitable that all the people
know the paintings.
Those who are subjects [the people]
will be corrupted
and the country will go astray,
because many lies are preserved there,
for many in the paintings
have been hailed as gods."[2]

The pre-Columbian man truly realized the significance of what we call history. Later examples that confirm this also show the techniques they used in their kind of historical literature. Just as in epic and other forms of poetry, here also the repetition of parallel phrases served a very important end. Although the chronicles and indigenous histories are considered as prose, they contain a certain rhythmic style which undoubtedly helped in memorizing. Scenes and events of the past are depicted in a somewhat critical manner, concisely and with fewer metaphors, while also including, in veiled form, myths and legends. Although it is often difficult to separate legend from history, in some ways

2 *Códice Matritense de la Real Academia*, VIII, fol. 192 v.

fantastic accounts may be considered historical, since they show traces of ancient forms of thinking and acting.

We will begin with the historical texts left by the Mayas, their chronicles and histories which were recorded after the Conquest in the indigenous language but in Latin script. From the Mayas of Yucatán there are three of these chronicles originally included in the *Chilam Balam* books of Maní, Tizimín, and Chumayel. The well-known researcher, Juan Pío Pérez, very early took note of the parallel portions in these three manuscripts. The correlation of these historical sections done by Professor Barrera Vásquez clearly shows the nature of this ancient form of Maya chronicle.[3] Memories of the past are presented schematically, accompanied only by the corresponding dates.

Here is a brief summary of the content of these chronicles. The first part covers the migrations of the Tutul-Xiuh groups up to their arrival in the northern part of the Yucatan Peninsula in the ninth and tenth centuries A.D. The second part refers to the wanderings of the Itzás and their return to Chichén Itzá; mention is also made of the struggles between the city-states of Chichén Itzá, Mayapán, and Uxmal in northern Yucatán. The last part deals with the arrival of the Spaniards and the colonial period up to the beginning of the seventeenth century. The following is a translation of the first part of the correlated text which tells of the migrations of the Tutul-Xiuhs:

This is the order of the *ḳatúns,*
from the time the Xiuhs left their lands,
their houses in Nonohual.
During four *ḳatúns,*
they were west of Suyúa.
The land from where they came
is Tulapan Chiconauhtlan.
Four *ḳatúns*
they walked until they arrived here.
Leading them was Chantepeu
and his companions.
When they left that region,

[3] *The Maya Chronicles.*

it was the 8-Ahau Katún [928–48 A.D.].
It is the 6-Ahau Katún [948–68 A.D.].
It is the 4-Ahau Katún [968–87 A.D.].
It is the 2-Ahau Katún [987–1007 A.D.].
Four year-counts and one year more (81 years),
it was the year 1-Tun [1-Stone]
of the 13-Ahau Katún [1007–27 A.D.].
They arrived in this region.
Four year-counts and one more
they had wandered
since they left their lands
to arrive in this region
of Chacnabiton. . . .[4]

This fragment translated from the Maya shows how precise chronologically and yet extremely succinct were the old chronicles invented to
preserve from oblivion the main thread of significant events in the life
of a people.

Later, because of the systematic memorizing of tradition in their
schools, the Mayas began to elaborate the early schematic accounts, en-
riching them with many details and anecdotes which gave a more human
touch to their chronicles. Good examples of this are found in some passages of the *Chilam Balam* books, the *Popol Vuh* of the Quichés, the
Annals of the Cakchiquels, and various other manuscripts. A sample of
this elaborated form of history is a story from the *Popol Vuh* about the
arrival of the Quichés at what was to be their capital, Gumarcaah, known
in Náhuatl texts as Utatlán:

> After a long journey, they came here to the city of Guymarcaah, the
> name which the Quichés gave it when the kings Cotuhá and Gucumatz
> and all the lords came. They had entered then in the fifth generation of
> men since the population began to grow and had a more cultured life, the
> beginning of the existence of our nation. Many made their houses there
> and at the same time constructed the temple of the god; in the center of the
> high part of the city they put it, when they arrived and established
> themselves.

[4] *Ibid.*, 26–28.

question of the ethnical identity.

121

Then came the increase of their power. They were many and numerous when they held a council meeting in their great house. They came together and they separated, because dissension arose and there was jealousy among them, for the price of their sisters and their daughters, and because they no longer drank together. This then was the cause wherefore they were divided and some turned against others and they threw out the skulls of each other's dead, the ones and the others threw them out.

Then they divided into nine families and, being finished the contention over the sisters and the daughters, they carried out a division of the realm into twenty-four great houses, and thus it was done. It was a long time ago that they all came there to the city, when the twenty-four great houses were finished, there in the city of Gumarcaah. . . .

There they increased; there they installed with splendor their thrones and seats of honor, and rank was established among all the lords. They were nine families with nine lords of Cavec; nine with lords of Nihaib; four with lords of Ahau-Quiché and two with lords of Zaquic.

They became again very numerous and many also were those who followed each lord; those were the first of their vassals, and many were the families of each lord.[5]

Another example among the many that could be transcribed to show how historical accounts were phrased and elaborated is provided by the *Annals of the Cakchiquels*. It describes in vivid imagery the fight with much bloodshed between the Cakchiquels and the Quichés in the middle of the fifteenth century. The extract given here tells of the Quiché march to the city of Iximchée, capital of the Cakchiquel nation, the meeting of the Cakchiquel council of chieftains, and their methods of defense. All is described with true mastery, including the battle itself in which the aggressive Quichés were finally defeated:

The arrival of the Quichés at Iximchée was on the day 10-Tzíi. Our grandfathers, Oxlahuh Tzíi and Cablahub Tihax, did not know that the Quichés were coming to kill the Zotzils and Tukuchés. Only a fugitive who heard the news brought it to the kings. "Day after tomorrow they will kill you. They have come to annihilate all, the Quichés, to kill the people in the city, where they will go in. Truly, it is frightening to see how they

[5] *Popol Vuh*, 215–17. Quiché text, 150–52.

122

come. They are not eight or sixteen thousand men." Thus said the fugitive when he came to the Cakchiquels.

The lords immediately came together in council and said: "Now you have heard; it is necessary to cut the path of the Quichés." This the kings said. At once they went out to occupy the road; a division of soldiers went forth to cut the Quichés to pieces. Only the people in the city went out to this meeting. They took the main road; they went also towards the summit of the mountain and took a stand to engage the enemy, those of Tibakoy and Raxakán, and they closed the roadway to those of Galeah, Pazaki, Uleuh, and Ginona.

Immediately the warriors inspected their shields and weapons of war, waiting for the arrival of the enemy.

When the sun appeared on the horizon and its light fell on the mountain, the outcry and shouts of war broke forth, banners were unfurled, and the big flutes, drums, and conch shells resounded. It was indeed terrible when the Quichés arrived. But with great speed they [the Cakchiquels] went down to surround them, concealing themselves so as to form a circle; and arriving at the foot of the hill, they went close to the banks of the river, cutting off the river houses from the servants of the kings Tepépul and Ixtáyul who were accompanying their god. Immediately was the encounter. Truly the contest was terrible. The outcries resounded, the shouts of war, the flutes, the drums, and the conch shells; then the warriors performed their acts of magic. Quickly the Quichés were defeated; they ceased to fight and were dispersed, annihilated and dead. It was impossible to count the dead.

As a result, the kings Tepépul and Ixtáyul were conquered and made prisoners. They yielded themselves and gave up their god. In this way Galel Achí, Ahpop Achí, the grandson and son of a king, Ahxit, Ahpuvak, Ahtzib, and Ahqot and all the warriors were destroyed and executed. They could not be estimated as eight or sixteen thousand, the Quichés that the Cakchiquels killed on that occasion. Thus our fathers and grandfathers recount, oh my sons! This is what they did, the kings Oxlahuh Tzíi and Cablahuh Tihax together with Voo Ymox and Dokel Batzín. And in no other way was Iximchée made great. . . .[6]

This vigorous picture of the gory encounter, with the music of drums

---

[6] *Memorial de Tecpan-Atitlan, (Anales de los Cakchiqueles),* ed. by J. Antonio Villacorta, 106–10.

and conch shells and the acts of magic by warriors, brings out clearly the literary sensitivity of a people who well remembered their past. Their insistence on giving exact dates when each event occurred shows once more their concern to place all happenings within the continuing frame of time. As the last chapter of this book explains, some wise men who lived through the Conquest also were concerned to pass on the memory of their last struggle against the Spanish conquerors who were bringing to an end their culture and ancient way of life. In fact, the native records of the Conquest are dramatic proof of the persistence of what can be called a deeply rooted historical consciousness.

What was true in the case of the Maya was much the same in the case of Náhuatl wise men and chroniclers. The text quoted at the beginning of this chapter, in which the Aztec historian Tezozómoc tells of the manner in which the memory of the Náhuatl past was handed down from generation to generation, serves as an introduction to the study of Náhuatl history. Further light is thrown on their history by an ancient legend about what might be called the Náhuatl rediscovery of history. The legend tells of the arrival, in the distant past, of wise men who brought with them books of paintings and a knowledge of the arts. They came to the mythical Tamoanchan, "the place of our origin." But one day, in obedience to an inspiration from their god, they set out to march towards the east, towards the region of the immense waters. After the wise men had left, those who stayed behind, the common people, realized that they no longer had their ancient wisdom, that they had been deprived of their means of keeping alive the memory of the past. There was a great outcry, for they feared they had lost the light which showed them the way:

Will the sun shine, will it dawn?
How will the people move,
how will they stand?
For they have gone away, they have carried off
the black and red ink, the painted books.
How will the people exist?
How will the earth continue, the city?

How will there be stability?
Who is it that will govern us?
Who is it that will guide us?
Who is it that will show us the way?
What will be our standard?
What will be our measure?
What will be our pattern?
From where should we begin?
What will be our torch, our light?[7]

In the midst of the confusion they found some old men whose advice was to prove all important. They were four wise men who had not wanted to go away. Their names were Tlaltetecuin, Xochicahuaca, Oxomoco and Cipactónal. At the insistence of the people, the four old ones came together and after long deliberation succeeded in rediscovering the ancient wisdom, the ancient form of preserving the memory of their past:

Then they rediscovered the count of the days,
the annals and the year-count,
the book of dreams;
they ordained it as it had been kept,
and as it has continued,
the time that endured the domain of the Toltecs,
the domain of the Tepanecs,
the domain of the Mexicans,
and all the Chichimec domains.[8]

Whether all myth or partly true, this is the account, the dramatic picture of the efforts of a people not to lose the memory of their deeds. The indigenous text telling of the ancient Náhuatl rediscovery of history speaks for itself. For the Nahuas the black and red ink of the codices was the light and the measure which made it possible for them to find their way and for the city and even the earth itself to continue to exist. In the old records, in the books of the years, was the torch which illuminated and which converted the earth, populated with gods, into a cosmic home for the people. The endless struggle continued. There was suffering and

[7] *Códice Matritense de la Real Academia*, fol. 192 v.
[8] *Loc. cit.*

restlessness in the world, but at least the people could search for a meaning in life.

Like the Mayas, the people of Central Mexico also had an early form of chronicle, recorded principally in an ideographic script in their codices. They set down schematically the most important deeds which should be remembered. Transcribed here from the various texts that survive is a brief section of the Aztec document known as *Codex Aubin*. It speaks of the pilgrimage of the ancient Mexicans, their passage by the mountain of Coatépetl and their arrival at Tula and various other places:

Year 2-House:
here for the first time was made the "binding of years" [cycle of 52 years].
On the hill of Coatépetl the fire was lighted, in the year 2-Reed.
In the year 3-Flint:
the Mexicans arrived at Tula.
In the year 9-Reed:
the Mexicans had been twenty years in Tula.
Year 10-Flint:
they arrived at Atlitlalaquian.
There they remained eleven years.
In the year 8-Reed they came to Tlemaco.
In Tlemaco they remained five years.
In the year 13-Flint:
they arrived at Atotonilco.
Four years the Mexicans remained in Atotonilco. . . .[9]

This manner of connecting events and dates, very similar to that found in the Maya chronicles and in the codices of other groups such as the Mixtecs, seems to be an intimate part of the most ancient style of indigenous history. And, again like the Mayas, the Náhuatl-speaking people gave further meaning to their history by commentaries which accompanied the content of their codices. Inserted into these commentaries which were learned in the schools were many descriptions showing the life and activities of the governors and people at different periods. For-

[9] *Códice Aubin*, in Antonio Peñafiel, *Colección de Documentos para la Historia Mexicana*, 17–22.

tunately, some of these records are preserved, written down soon after the Conquest with Latin script in the native language. Among these are the manuscript known as *Códice Chimalpopoca,* which includes the *Anales de Cuauhtitlán;* the *Anales históricos de la nación mexicana,* written down by wise men of Tlatelolco; some sections of the already mentioned *Codex Aubin;* and others. There are also many texts of a historical nature which were written down at the end of the sixteenth and the beginning of the seventeenth centuries by a group of native or mestizo historians who wished to make their ancient culture and traditions known to the Spanish world.

In the *Anales de Cuauhtitlán* and in some texts by the native informants of Sahagún are preserved the ancient accounts, myths, and legends of the Toltec greatness and of the culture hero Quetzalcóatl. They tell about the great prince, creator of the arts and prosperity of the Toltecs. Here is a fragment of a native text:

Year 1-Reed:
it is said, it is told,
in this year was born Quetzalcóatl,
he who was called Our Prince,
the priest 1-Reed, Quetzalcóatl.
It is said that his mother
was called Chimalman.
And thus it is told
how Quetzalcóatl was placed
in the womb of his mother:
she swallowed a precious stone. . . .
Years 2-Flint, 3-House,
4-Rabbit, 5-Reed,
6-Flint, 7-House,
8-Rabbit, 9-Reed.
In 9-Reed, Quetzalcóatl asked about his father.
He was already nine years old,
he had reached the age of discernment.
He said:
"I would like to know my father,
to know his face."

They replied to him:
"He died; out there they buried him."
Forthwith Quetzalcóatl went
to dig in the earth;
he looked for the bones of his father. . . .[10]

In this way was recorded the portentous origin of Quetzalcóatl. On the one hand, it was stated that his mother Chimalman became pregnant by magic; on the other hand, it was suggested that he might have had a father, the famous Mixcóatl. The same text continues and says that at twenty-seven years of age Quetzalcóatl went to the region of Tulancingo where he did penance for four years.

Year 2-Rabbit:
then arrived Quetzalcóatl
there in Tulancingo.
There he passed four years,
he built his house of penance,
his house of green crossbeams.
Then he went out through Cuextlan,
in that place he crossed a river;
for this he made a bridge.
They say that it still exists. . . .
In that year the Toltecs went to take
Quetzalcóatl,
that he should govern them
there in Tula
and also be their priest. . . .[11]

Then began Quetzalcóatl's creative work as ruler and priest of the Toltecs. It is said, among other things, that the great priest discovered the supreme mystery of divinity:

And it is told, it is said,
that Quetzalcóatl invoked
Someone who was deified,
in the innermost of heaven:

[10] *Anales de Cuauhtitlán*, fol. 3–4.
[11] *Loc. cit.*

She of the starry skirt.
He who makes things shine;
Lady of our flesh, Lord of our flesh;
She who supports the earth,
He who covers it with cotton.
Toward that place he directed his plea,
thus it was known;
toward the Place of Duality,
above the nine levels of heaven.
And it was known that
he invoked the One who dwelt there,
made supplications,
living in meditation and retirement. . . .[12]

Some of the texts cited in the chapter on epic poetry give a marvelous picture of the Toltec world where all was abundance because of the wisdom of Quetzalcóatl. But this prosperity came to a sudden end because Quetzalcóatl did not want to betray his religious belief. Wizards came to Tula and disturbed the people, even the great priest himself. The following text in the *Anales de Cuauhtitlán* tells of this:

They say that when Quetzalcóatl lived there,
often the wizards tried to trick him
into offering human sacrifices,
into sacrificing men.
But he never did, because he loved his people
who were the Toltecs. . . .
And they say, they relate,
that this angered the magicians
so that they began to scoff at him,
to make fun of him.
The magicians and wizards said
they wanted to torment him
so that finally he would go away,
as it really happened.
In the year 1-Reed, Quetzalcóatl died.
Truly they say

[12] *Loc. cit.*

Amazing combination of myth and history

that he went to die there,
in the Land of the Black and Red Color.[13]

This form of narration, based on a more or less mythical chronology, seems to be an intermediate step between legend and history. But while the ancient annals preserve legends such as this one about Quetzalcóatl, they also contain descriptions of actual incidents in everyday life which are intensely human. An example of this is the intervention by the lord, Quinatzin, King of Cuauhtitlán, in behalf of the Aztecs when they were overpowered in Chapultepec. Quinatzin ordered his warriors to free the captive Aztecs held prisoner by the people of Xaltocan. Among the captives was the young girl Chimallaxóchitl, a Mexican princess, daughter of Huitzilihuitzin. Quinatzin did not realize that she was to be his companion and wife:

When the lord Quinatzin learned that the Mexicans had been overpowered, he commanded that those of Xaltocan who imprisoned them in Chapultepec should be pursued. He ordered that the captured Mexicans should be freed by force. Thus it was done. When the lord Quinatzin obliged those to set them free, there was captive of those of Xaltocan a young Mexican girl named Chimallaxóchitl, daughter of Huitzilihuitzin who had ruled in Chapultepec. . . .

The young girl was brought to Tepetlapan before the face of the lord Quinatzin. On seeing her, he loved her. He wanted to go to her side and have access to her. But she did not consent. She said to him: "This is not possible now, my lord. I am in the time of ritual fast. Afterwards it will be as you wish. . . . For two years now I am fulfilling my promise and in two years more I will have finished. Command, my lord, that they make me an oratory. There I will put my sacred vessel and I will make offerings to my god. There I will fast."

Immediately Lord Quinatzin gave the order. An oratory was erected on the south of Tequixquináhuac and Huitznáhuac. When the oratory was built, they took the young girl there. She fasted there.

When the fast was finished, the lord Quinatzin married her. The princess bore a child and she said: "Go and tell the king that a child is born. He should give it a name."

13 *Ibid.*, fol. 10.

The offering at the temple (above) and musicians and singers (below). *Codex Florentine.*

"Admonitions of the Aztec lords"—a page of *Códice Matritense del Real Palacio* (texts of the native informants of Sahagún).

Lord Quinatzin, being informed, gave a name to his son. He said: "His name shall be Tlazanótztoc, 'the arrow made a noise.' " When the mother knew this she said: "He is called thus because the king engendered him where he was hunting, in his hunting field."

When his child was born, Lord Quinatzin ordered, informed all the Chichimec lords, that henceforth they would not be friends with the people of Xaltocan, that those should never live at his side.... The princess, daughter of the Mexicans, later had her second child. Lord Quinatzin did not tell her what was to be his name. She alone gave it to him, and named him Tezcateuhtli, "lord of the mirror," a title of her god Tezcatlipoca. The young girl, since she was a captive, had always kept with her a mirror so that she could arrange her hair. She also had a green mantle ... The name of her first son, called Tlazanótztoc, was not pleasing to her. For this reason she alone gave the second child his name. This one later was king of Cuauhtitlán....[14]

There are many narrations such as this in the annals of the Náhuatl world—simple and with a touch of human interest. They show that indigenous history had passed through the stage of schematic chronicle which carried only the notation of principal events accompanied by dates. Other accounts similar to this one about the king and the princess are listed in the bibliography at the end of this book. Some of these stories and descriptions might be called "imaginative prose," works of creative fantasy in which the author enlivens the universe of chronicle and tradition. The following chapter will consider this type of narration along with other forms of prose which were common not only in pre-Hispanic times, but are found also today among indigenous groups.

The last chapter of this book presents and comments upon further selections of historical texts, translated from the Náhuatl and Maya languages, which show the viewpoint of the vanquished people immediately after the Spanish Conquest and how the surviving wise men interpreted their own fall and the destruction of their culture and ancient ways of life.

[14] *Ibid.*, fol. 13–14.

VI

Other Forms of Prose

THE RICH WORLD OF PRE-COLUMBIAN PROSE includes not only chronicles and history but also descriptions and narrative texts, speeches, and admonitions. Naturally it is sometimes difficult to determine the exact nature of a given composition. Often there are texts which appear to be imaginative prose included as part of a chronicle. Or what seems to be a straightforward speech or admonition sometimes holds to a rhythm which suggests poetry. Certainly it would be a mistake to apply indiscriminately to indigenous productions the classifications originally appropriate to western literature. Therefore some of these literary categories are used merely as a matter of expediency. The texts presented in this chapter are divided into two main groups: imaginative prose and didactic prose.

Imaginative prose includes descriptions and narrations which are more or less legendary, sometimes similar to the ancient tales and fables found in other literatures. This form of narration is still very popular among contemporary native groups, which probably indicates that it was also common in more ancient times. As in the case of historic prose, these stories and narrations follow many of the stylistic procedures which are frequent in other forms of pre-Hispanic composition, such as the parallel expressions which repeat the same idea in different ways, the often observed rhythm of phrases, and the constant use of metaphors and idiomatic expressions, undeniable characteristics of these indigenous languages.

Didactic prose, of which even more examples can be found, includes the famous *huehuetlatolli,* or discourses of the elders, and many other compositions memorized in the schools and private homes. These contain the ancient religious and moral doctrines, the rules by which the people lived, their manner of behavior. Besides this, there is a form of prose which describes the various cultural institutions: the organization of trade and courts of justice, the qualities and comportment proper to a priest, the calendar and ceremonies. There also are texts which tell of the knowledge of the animal world, of plants, medicines, and even of what might be described as the entire world of nature. Náhuatl literature is rich in examples of this kind of prose. The Mayas and even some other groups such as the Tarascans, to whom we are indebted for the well-known *Relación de Michoacán,* have also left evidence of their creations in this form of expression.

Let us begin with the prose texts from the Náhuatl world. A good example of their imaginative prose is the narration preserved in Tezozómoc's *Crónica Mexicáyotl,* which tells how the king, Huitzilíhuitl, succeeded in taking as wife the daughter of the lord of Cuauhnáhuac. A reading of the text makes it clear that, although it may contain a certain historical basis, it is principally legend, a successful blending of fantasy and facts. The adventures of the Aztec lord, Huitzilíhuitl, as he confronted the objections of the lord of Cuauhnáhuac, who was determined not to give his daughter as wife, are colorfully painted:

> Huitzilíhuitl, in the proper manner, wanted to make wife the princess named Miahuaxíhuitl, daughter of the king of Cuauhnáhuac, whose name was Ozomatzinteuctli.
>
> As the elders tell it, the domains of Ozomatzinteuctli were made up of the natives of Cuauhnáhuac, who brought him a large quantity of cotton as well as a great variety of fruits which grew there. None of these fruits were brought to Mexico, nor did cotton come to the Mexicans, for which reason they were in great misery; only a few Mexicans dressed in cotton, and a few others wore a *máxtlatl* [support] made of *amoxtli,* which grew in the water.
>
> For this reason Huitzilíhuitl, king of the Mexicans, sent to ask for the princess of Cuauhnáhuac as wife. He had said repeatedly: "How can we become related to Ozomatzinteuctli, the lord of Cuauhnáhuac? Why, by asking the king for his daughter for me!" As they say, Huitzilíhuitl had

investigated carefully beforehand in all directions, but he did not want anything from anywhere else. His heart went out only to Cuauhnáhuac, for which reason he sent the elders immediately to ask for the princess as wife.

As they say, Ozomatzinteuctli was a magician, a *nahualli*. He called all the spiders and also the centipedes, the serpents, the bats, and the scorpions; he ordered them to guard his young daughter, Miahuaxíhuitl, who was very beautiful, so that no one should come where she was and no one should dishonor her. The young girl was shut in and well protected, with every kind of wild beast guarding her at all the doors of the palace; because of this there was very great fear and no one came near the palace. Lords from all parts asked for this princess Miahuaxíhuitl, because they wanted to marry their sons to her, but Ozomatzinteuctli did not accept any offer.

It has been said that Huitzilíhuitl had his elders look carefully in all places: in Chalco, even in Tepanecapan although he had already chosen one of his concubines there, and also in such places as Aculhuacan, Culhuacan, Cuitláhuac, and Xochimilco.

One night Yoalli [the god Tezcatlipoca] spoke to Huitzilíhuitl in a dream, saying to him: "We will enter Cuauhnáhuac in spite of the people; we will go to the house of Ozomatzinteuctli and we will take his daughter, who is called Miahuaxíhuitl."

As soon as Huitzilíhuitl wakened, he sent immediately to Cuauhnáhuac to ask for the princess as wife. When Ozomatzinteuctli heard the speech with which the Mexicans asked for his daughter, he merely turned to them and said: "What is Huitzilíhuitl saying? What can he give her? That which grows in the water? And just as he is seen with a *máxtlatl* of *amoxtli* from the muddy water, would he dress her thus? And what will he give her to eat? Or perhaps that place is like this one, where there is everything, food and all different fruits, the necessary cotton, and rich apparel? Go tell all this to your king, Huitzilíhuitl before you come here again!"

Immediately after this the marriage makers came to tell Huitzilíhuitl that Ozomatzinteuctli did not consent to give his daughter. Huitzilíhuitl was very distressed to learn that his request had not been granted.

Again in a dream Yoalli spoke to him saying: "Do not despair, for I come to tell you what you must do to have Miahuaxíhuitl. Make a dart and a net. With these you will go hunting; you will throw the dart at the house of Ozomatzinteuctli, where his daughter is confined as if she were a beautiful reed. Adorn your dart carefully and paint it well, placing in the center a precious stone, a very precious stone with beautiful colors. You will go there to her place, where you will cast the dart with the precious stone; it has to fall there where the daughter of Ozomatzinteuctli is confined. And then we will have her."

This the king, Huitzilíhuitl did, betaking himself to the place of Cuauhnáhuac; and immediately he cast the dart, well painted and well made, inside which was the precious stone as already mentioned, with beautiful colors. It fell in the middle of the patio where the young girl, Miahuaxíhuitl, was confined.

When the dart fell in the middle of the patio, the young girl Miahuaxíhuitl saw it come down from the sky. And, as they say, instantly she took it in her hand and looked at it, marveling and admiring the many different colors she had never seen before. Then she broke it in the middle and she saw the already mentioned extraordinary stone with beautiful colors, which she took out, saying to herself: "Is it hard?" She put it in her mouth, she swallowed, it went down, and she could not get it out; with this began her pregnancy and the future king Motecuhzoma Ilhuicaminatzin was conceived. . . .[1]

This delightful example of imaginative prose is only a sample; the door is open for researchers to study and translate similar compositions. In these, as in poetry, is revealed the creative sensitivity of the "masters of the word" in pre-Hispanic Mexico.

There are also many examples of Náhuatl didactic prose, among which are the royal proclamations and discourses on such solemn occasions as birth, marriage, and death and the advice of parents to their children found in the various collections of *huehuetlatolli* or discourses of the elders, which, as Fray Bernardino de Sahagún has already noted, might be said to contain the most profound wisdom of the ancient Mexicans. A specimen of this form of literature is the following complete version of a father's counsel to his young daughter when she comes of age.

The words of the Náhuatl father describe to his child the condition of man on earth. Here is the place of painful pleasure, but although there are few things that bring satisfaction and pleasure, one does not always

[1] Tezozómoc, *op. cit.*, 90–95.

have to be complaining about this. Each person must fulfill his destiny on earth as imposed by the Supreme Being, the Lord of the Close and the Near. The young girl must realize her own destiny, and that is why her father tells her how to act. He shows her in detail what she must do during the daytime, how she must train herself in what are the proper duties of women: spinning, weaving, and the preparation of food and drink. Finally, he also tells his daughter how to behave in every circumstance, especially impressing on her the ancient principles concerning sexual morality. The translation offered here attempts to preserve the characteristic Náhuatl form of expression, with its often mentioned parallelisms and its unmistakable rhythm and metaphors.

Here you are, my little girl, my necklace of precious stones, my plumage, my human creation, born of me. You are my blood, my color, my image.

Now listen, understand. You are alive, you have been born; Our Lord, the Master of the Close and the Near, the maker of people, the inventor of men, has sent you to earth.

Now that you begin to look around you, be aware. Here it is like this: there is no happiness, no pleasure. There is heartache, worry, fatigue. Here springs up and grows suffering and distress.

Here on earth is the place of much wailing, the place where our strength is worn out, where we are well acquainted with bitterness and discouragement. A wind blows, sharp as obsidian it slides over us.

They say truly that we are burned by the force of the sun and the wind. This is the place where one almost perishes of thirst and hunger. This is the way it is here on earth.

Listen well, my child, my little girl. There is no place of well-being on the earth, there is no happiness, no pleasure. They say that the earth is the place of painful pleasure, of grievous happiness.

The elders have always said: "So that we should not go round always moaning, that we should not be filled with sadness, the Lord has given us laughter, sleep, food, our strength and fortitude, and finally the act by which men propagate."

All this sweetens life on earth so that we are not always moaning. But even though it be like this, even though it be true that there is only suffering and this is the way things are on earth, even so, should we always be afraid? Should we always be fearful? Must we live weeping?

But see, there is life on the earth, there are the lords; there is authority, there is nobility, there are eagles and tigers [knights]. And who is always saying that so it is on earth? Who goes about trying to put an end to his life? There is ambition, there is struggle, work. One looks for a wife, one looks for a husband.

But now, my little one, listen well, look carefully: here is your mother, our lady, from whose bosom, from whose womb you appeared, you came forth. As the leaf opens, so you grew, you flowered, as if you had been sleeping and awakened.

Listen, look, understand, for thus it is on earth. Do not be idle, do not walk aimlessly, do not wander without a destination. How should you live? How should you go on for a short time? They say it is very difficult to live on the earth, a place of terrific struggle, my little lady, my little bird, my little one.

Be careful, because you come from a renowned family, you descend from them, you are born from illustrious people. You are the thorn, the offshoot of our lords. The lords have left us, those who governed; they are standing in line there, those who came to take command in the world; they gave renown and fame to the nobility.

Listen. Much do I want you to understand that you are noble. See that you are very precious, even while you are still only a little lady. You are a precious stone, you are a turquoise. You have been formed, shaped; you have the blood, the color; you are the offshoot and the stem; you are a descendant of noble lineage.

And now I am going to tell you this. Perhaps you do not understand very well? Are you still playing with earth and potsherds? Perhaps you are still sitting on the ground? Truly, you must listen a little for you already understand these things; by yourself you are gaining experience.

See that you do not dishonor yourself and our lords, the princes, the governors who preceded us. Do not act like the common people of the village, do not become an ordinary person. As long as you live on the earth, near and close to the people, be always a true little lady.

Look now at your work, that which you have to do: during night and day, devote yourself to the things of God; think often how He is like the night and the wind. Pray to Him, invoke Him, call to Him, beg Him earnestly when you are in the place where you sleep. This way your sleep will be pleasant.

Waken, get up in the middle of the night, prostrate yourself on your knees and your elbows, raise your neck and your shoulders. Invoke Him, call the Lord, our Lord, He who is as the night and the wind. He will be merciful, He will hear you in the night, He will look upon you with compassion; then He will grant you your destiny, what is set aside for you.

And if the destiny should be bad, the portion which they gave you when it was still night, what came with you at birth, when you came into life, with this supplication it will be made good, rectified; the Lord will change it, our Lord, the Master of the Close and Near.

Watch for the dawn, get up quickly, extend your hands, extend your arms, raise your face, wash your hands, cleanse your mouth, take up the broom quickly, begin to sweep. Do not be idle, do not stay there close to the fire; wash the mouths of your little brothers; burn copal incense, do not forget it, for thus you will have the mercy of Our Lord.

And this being done, when you will be prepared, what will you do? How will you fulfill your womanly duties? Will you not prepare the food, the drink? Will you not spin and weave? Look well how are the food and drink, how they are made, that they should be good; know how good food and good drink are prepared.

These things that are sometimes called "things appropriate for persons of distinction," they are the duty of the wives of those who govern; for this they are called things that belong to the nobles, the food proper for one who governs, his drink. Be skillful in preparing the drink, in preparing the food. Pay attention, dedicate yourself, apply yourself to see how this is done; thus life will pass, thus you will be at peace. Thus you will be highly esteemed. Let it be not in vain if Our Lord some time may send you misfortune. Sometimes there is poverty among the nobles. Face it; then take hold of it, for this is the duty of a woman: spinning and weaving.

Open well your eyes to see what is the Toltec art, what is the art of feathers; how to embroider in colors and how to interweave the threads; how women dye them, those who are like you, our wives, the noble women. How they place the threads on the loom, how to make the woof of the cloth, how to hold it fast. Pay attention, apply yourself, be not idle, do not stand idly by, be strict with yourself.

Now is the right time, there is still plenty of time, because there is still jade in your heart, turquoise. It is still fresh, it has not been spoiled, it has not been altered, nothing has twisted it. We are still here, we your parents, who have brought you here to suffer; because in this way the world continues. Thus it is said, thus the word was given, thus Our Lord arranged it, so that there should be always, there should be offspring on the earth.

We are still here, it is still our time, not yet has come the stick and the stone of Our Lord. We are not yet dead, we have not perished. Of what are you thinking, child, little bird, little one? When Our Lord will have hidden us, you will be cared for by another, for it is not your destiny, it was not meant for you to sell vegetables, wood, handfuls of chili, pots of salt, *tesquesquite* stone, standing at the doorways of the houses, because you are noble. Learn to spin, to weave, to prepare food and drink.

May no one's heart ever become disdainful of you, say anything about you, point a finger at you, talk about you. If things come out badly, how will you react to misfortune? Because of this will we be blamed? When Our Lord will have taken us to Himself, will we be reprimanded in the Region of the Dead? But as for you, do not put into motion the stick and the stone against yourself. Do not cause them to come against you.

But even if you are attentive, cannot censure fall upon you? And if you are praised too much by others, let not your countenance become proud, do not act as if you had the rank of eagle or tiger, as if you held Huitzilopochtli's shield in your hand, as if it were due to you that our heads are raised, that our countenances are magnified. But if you do nothing, then will you not be like a block of stone? They will not speak of you, you will have little praise. Be and act according to what Our Lord wishes for you.

Look now at something else which I want to impress on you, communicate to you, my human creation, my little daughter. Do not permit the lords from whom you are born to be mocked. Do not throw dust or rubbish on them; do not cast any uncleanness on their history, on their black and red ink, on their fame.

Do not insult them in any way, such as wanting things of this earth, such as seeking to enjoy them out of season, those which are called sexual things. And if you do not withdraw from them, can you ever come near the gods? Better that you should perish immediately.

So now calmly, very calmly, pay attention; if thus Our Lord sees it, if someone should speak of you, if they should say something about you, do not scorn it, do not kick with your foot what may be an inspiration of Our Lord; take it up; do not withdraw so that it would have to come back to you two or three times. Even though you be our very daughter, because you are born of us, do not become proud, forgetting Our Lord in your heart. For thus you will fall into the dust and rubbish, which is the life of public women. And then Our Lord will scoff at you, will do with you as He chooses.

Do not seek him who will be your companion as if in a market place; do not call to him as if you were aflame in the springtime, do not go about desiring him. But also, take care not to disdain the one who may be your companion, the one chosen by the Lord. For if you look down on him, it might be that Our Lord would scoff at you, and finally you might become as a public woman.

But prepare yourself; watch who is your enemy so that no one should make light of you. Do not give yourself to a wastrel, to one who seeks you for his own pleasure, a depraved boy. Nor should two or three faces you may have seen know you. Whoever may be your companion, you two must go to the end of life together. Do not leave him, hold to him, cling to him even though he be a poor man, even though he be only a small eagle, a small tiger, an unhappy soldier, a poor noble, sometimes tired, lacking goods; not for that do you neglect him.

May Our Lord look upon you, may He strengthen you, He who knows man, the Inventor of people, the Maker of human beings.

With these words from my mouth do I give all this to you. Thus before Our Lord, I fulfill my duty. And if perchance you cast this away, still you know it. I have fulfilled my duty, my little woman, my little daughter. May you be happy, may Our Lord bring you success.[2]

The father's admonition to his little daughter has covered every aspect of life. His wise and profound words are an excellent example of Náhuatl instructive literature. Speeches and conversations similar to this were pronounced not only in the homes but also in the schools where students received the very essence of their ancient cultural legacy. Sahagún's informants rescued several of these texts, which are really lessons on human nature, the surrounding world, and the gods. The hundreds of folios of the *Matritense* and *Florentine codices* are the principal sources of this literature, the greater part of which is in prose, and two further examples are taken from them. The first is concerned with the manner in which sacred rites were performed. It explains how the sun was honored at different times of the day and night:

Every day as the sun rises, quail are sacrificed and incense burned. And

[2] *Códice Florentino*, Book VI, fol. 74 v. ff.

this is how they sacrifice the quail: they cut their necks and raise them up as an offering to the sun. They address him, they say to him:

"The sun has risen, he who gives warmth, the precious child, the eagle which rises; how will he go on his way? How will he make the day? Perhaps something will happen to us who are his tail, his wings?"

They say to him:

"Deign to fulfill your function, to complete your mission, our lord." And this is said each day when the sun rises.

And how is incense offered? Four times during the day and five times during the night. The first time is when the sun has already risen, the second when it is lunch time, the third when the sun is halfway, and the fourth when it is about to set.

During the night they offer incense in this manner: the first time as it grows dark, the second at the time of going to bed, the third when the flute sounds, the fourth at midnight, and the fifth near dawn.

And when they offer copal at nightfall, they address the night, they say:

"The Lord of the Night has come to spread himself out, he of the sharp-pointed nose; how will his mission be accomplished?"[3]

A different kind of information is offered in the following text also taken from the *Códice Matritense*. It comes from an extremely interesting section of the codex, in which the Aztecs describe their various neighbors, other peoples with different languages and different ways of life. Here is what they thought of the Tarascans, the ancient inhabitants of Michoacán:

They are called Michuaque or "owners of fish"; this name is derived from the fact that fish are abundant in their land. They are also known as Quauochpanme, "those of the shaved head," because none of them let their hair grow. They all shave their heads, men and women, and also the old people. All are shaved. Only a very few allow their hair to grow.

In their land there is every kind of sustenance: maize, amaranth, kidney beans, sage, squash, and different fruits. Their manner of dress is as follows: the men use a kind of shirt without sleeves; they always carry their bows, their arrows; and their quivers they wear over the shoulder. They also dress in skins of the wildcat, the ocelot, bear, squirrel, deer. They adorn themselves with a round reddish-colored plumage which they wear on their heads attached to a band of squirrel hide.

[3] *Códice Matritense del Real Palacio*, fol. 271 v.

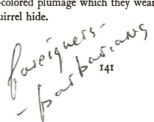

141

Their houses are very good, even though made entirely of straw. The Michuaques are artists in feather work, carpentry, wood carving, painting, and stone carving.

The women of the Michuaques are expert in spinning and weaving; they make thick mantles very skillfully. The men make very good sandals. When they prepare food, they make enough at one time for two or three days, even for eight days.

Here are the defects of the Michuaques: they do not use *máxtlatl* [a cloth to cover the private parts]. They just go uncovered. They are covered only with their shirt called *xicolli*, which is like a woman's *huipil* [chemise].

Also they make big perforations in their lips and their ears. Their earplugs and lip pendants are very large. The women wear skirts; they do not wear a chemise. Their skirts are not long; they only come to above the knees. Neither the women nor the men are especially expert in preparing food. . . .

The name of this people's god is Taras; because of him they are called Tarascans. This Taras is called in Náhuatl, Mixcóatl, god of the Chichimecs. They offer him serpents, birds, deer; they do not offer human sacrifices. They let their captives live; they make them their slaves. Their king is obeyed, respected; they obey him in all things. All pay him tribute, do him reverence. Their king or lord resembles the lord of Mexico.[4]

The above examples of prose show clearly the mark of those stylistic procedures so widely used in Náhuatl literary compositions. The extraordinary abundance of didactic and imaginative texts left by this culture invites us to delve more deeply into the thinking of the pre-Columbian priests and wise men.

Both Maya prose and Maya poetry, though similar in many respects to the creations of the Nahuas, have their own flavor and unique style of expression, among other things a distinct kind of native baroque symbolism. Maya imaginative prose, stories, and legends are also found among texts which often include many calendric references, genealogies, and historical accounts. This fusion of history and imagination is well illustrated by a document of Quiché origin known as "Titles from the House of Ixquin-Nehaib." It tells of the hand-to-hand fight, during the

---

[4] *Códice Matritense de la Real Academia*, fol. 190 r.–v.

Spanish Conquest, between Don Pedro de Alvarado and the Quiché lord, Tecum Umán.

The event took place in Pachah, on the plain of Pinal, near the town of Quetzaltenango. This was the decisive battle between the Quichés and the conquistadors. Although only an ancient Spanish translation of this document has survived, the original is known to have been recorded in the native language. Here is a literal version of the text:

And then the Spaniards began to fight with the ten thousand Indians who had with them this captain, Tecum. At first nothing happened; they only turned each other aside. Then they withdrew half a league and came together again. They fought three hours and the Spaniards killed many Indians. It was impossible to count how many were killed. Not a single Spaniard died; only the Indians, led by the captain, Tecum. Much blood was spilled from all the Indians that the Spaniards killed; and this happened in Pachah.

Then the captain Tecum appeared flying like an eagle; the eagle was covered with feathers which grew from it; they were not false; it had wings which grew from its body and it had three crowns; one was of gold, one of pearls, and one of diamonds and emeralds. This captain Tecum was determined to kill Tunadiú [Alvarado], who came riding on a horse; he struck the horse so as to strike Alvarado; and he cut off the horse's head with a bludgeon. It was not an iron bludgeon but a wooden one with obsidian knives; the captain Tecum did this by magic. And when he saw that he had not killed Alvarado but the horse, he returned again, flying like an eagle, so that from above he could kill Alvarado. Then Alvarado waited with his lance and ran it right through the middle of this captain, Tecum.

Then came two dogs; they did not have any hair, they were bald. These dogs seized the aforementioned Quiché to tear him to pieces; but as Alvarado saw that this Quiché who wore the three crowns of gold, silver, and diamonds and emeralds and pearls was very noble, he went to protect him from the dogs and he looked at him carefully. The Quiché was covered with quetzal and very beautiful plumage; and because of this, the name of this village is Quetzaltenango, the place defended by a quetzal bird, because here was the death of this captain Tecum. And then Alvarado called all his soldiers that they should come to see the beautiful Indian quetzal. Then he told his soldiers that he had never seen in Mexico, nor in Tlaxcala, nor in any of the villages he had conquered, an Indian so noble, such a prince, so covered with quetzal plumage and so handsome; and for that reason he said that the name of this village should be Quetzaltenango. Therefore this village has the name of Quetzaltenango.[5]

Maya instructive prose is found mainly in the *Chilam Balam* books. Fray Diego de Landa, speaking of the *Chilam* priests who were the authors of these works, said: "The duty of the priests was to study and to teach the sciences, and state what was needed and the remedy, to preach and to arrange the fiestas."[6] A brief example which gives an idea of the way celestial phenomena were described to the people appears in the book of *Chumayel*. It describes, in very general terms, an eclipse of the sun:

It appears to the people that there is a half circle on one side of the sun, as if a piece was bitten out. But here is what really happens. What has been bitten out is where it [the sun] has come abreast of the moon, which is pulled toward it until it bites into it. Then on its way northward it [this piece] becomes bigger until they are one, and the sun and the moon have eaten each other; then the sun becomes whole once more. This is the explanation given to the Maya people so they may know what happens to the sun and the moon.[7]

Examples of discourses and advice are found in chronicles such as the *Memorial de Tecpan-Atitlán*. From this Cakchiquel manuscript comes the following, a kind of prophecy spoken to groups of pilgrims during the long marches in search of what will be their own land. This exhortation, describing the difficulties which will beset them and also possibly bring them future glory, was probably transmitted from generation to generation as one of the literary legacies of this culture:

Great will be your burden; you will not sleep nor rest, but do not become discouraged, oh my children! You will be as rich, you will be as powerful as your bows, your shields allow. If you have given as tribute jade, metal, plumage, enchanting songs, by the same token they will be given to you; you will receive more than the others; you shall raise up

[5] "Títulos de la Casa de Ixquin-Nehaib," in *Crónicas Indígenas de Guatemala*, 89–90.
[6] *Op. cit.*, 123.
[7] Roys, *Chilam Balam of Chumayel*, 87. Maya text, 24.

higher your faces, because of the jade, the metal, the painted and carved objects which all the seven tribes have paid as tribute; there in those hills you shall raise up your faces. There will be a refuge for all of you; there you will raise up your bows, your shields. One will be your principal chief, and one will be he who follows him, from among you, the thirteen warriors, the thirteen princes. Soon you will raise up your faces and have your insignia, your bows, and your shields. There is war in the east, in the place called Zuiguá; there where you will go; there is the place for your shields which I will give to you, oh my children![8]

Texts such as this confirm the statement already made on the nature of pre-Columbian prose. Admonitions as well as tales and accounts are mingled in with chronicles, histories, and prophecies. It is certainly difficult to classify the various forms of native composition according to western literary categories.

From the Zapotecs of Oaxaca, unfortunately, there remain only some legends and narrations which have been repeated orally up to the present day. Therefore it is difficult in these narrations to separate those elements which are entirely pre-Hispanic from those which are a result of the many cultural exchanges during the centuries which have elapsed since the days of the Conquest. Such, for instance, is the case of a legend, gathered by Paul Radin in the village of Zaachila, which tells the story of the marriage of a daughter of the Aztec king, Ahuítzotl, to the great Zapotec lord, Cosijoeza.[9]

Transcribed here is a discourse preserved orally to the present day, which used to be pronounced by the elders when young couples were married. The content and also the rhythm of phrases recall similar admonitions found among other native groups, especially the Nahuas. The elder, speaking to the young couple and their families surrounding them, expresses himself in this manner:

In the dark night a breeze sighs; this is the most intense moment of life for young people. Our beloved divine mother presides over the feast which unites this couple. She has come with her countenance raised up, saying,

[8] *Anales de los Cakchiqueles*, 191.
[9] Radin, *An Historical Legend of the Zapotecas*.

"Oh, now you seek the glowing countenance! Oh, now you seek the splendor, guided by reason and sustained by heaven." It is thus one arrives at the mansion of the Lord. . . .

Now the sacred countenance has come here, the countenance, clear and shining within the heart of time. Now comes also new and clear sight of another road [the path of marriage].

As I come into the bosom of this family in my role of elder, it seems that another time is about to dawn, which is set aside in a broader realm, where night is hidden and there is only sincerity of hearts, where there arises the chorus of our ancestors. . . . As this couple is united, there comes the moment to penetrate into the very heart of their parentage. . . .

For this I implore the Lord, whom I worship, to make sacred the place where is spread out the palm sleeping mat for this young girl, this pure little virgin.

Oh, I came when the time was ripe, I came as a chief on the earth, representing the ancient holy men, so that you two should be united forever, should produce flowers, until you grow old [are prepared] for heaven. Hear my words, a gift of flowers, a sweet offering, with which I petition your happiness. . . .[10]

Discourses such as this, though collected in later times, give an insight into the style used in pre-Hispanic days. We may assume that probably there are similar compositions still in existence among other indigenous groups of contemporary Mexico.

From the Mixtecs, also in Oaxaca, who were the authors of several codices still in existence, comes a legend about the first time the sun appeared over the earth. This account, in the Mixtec language, has been carried by oral tradition up to recent times in various communities.

Appeared the day, the sun. A long time ago, in the beginning, there was no sun. Thus people lived in darkness. When at last the sun rose, many calamities occurred. Much music was heard. The sound of music came with the sun. There was much heat.

The people were very frightened. They dug deep pits and piled up stones around them. The people went into these holes and there they all perished. And those who died thus were called the unreligious people. And when thus they went into the holes, their dogs were changed into coyotes.

[10] Guillermo Orozco (ed.), *Tradiciones y Leyendas del Istmo de Tehuantepec*, 98–99.

Chronological account for the years 1385–99 in the Aztec *Codex Telleriano-Remensis.*

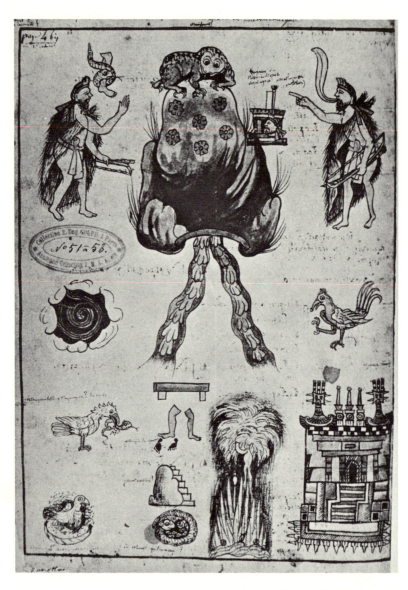

Arrival of the Toltecs at Tlachihualtépec. *Historia Tolteca-Chichi-meca* (*Annals of Cuauhtinchan*), 4.

For this reason there are coyotes up to now, because the dogs could not find any food to eat. They were changed into coyotes.

And the lizards went where the wolves were sleeping. The lizards did not have shirts to cover themselves. The wolves said to them: "Weave for yourselves shirts." But the lizards replied: "Tomorrow, tomorrow." Thus they said, and this is the way they always replied. And then the sun arrived at the zenith. The shoulders of the lizards became very hard. They were to blame, because they did not hurry to weave their shirts.[11]

The very ingenuousness of stories such as this which are recollections of the ancient cosmic myths shows clearly their popular origin. Anyone who studies other prose texts of these native cultures will discover surprisingly interesting and beautiful stories.

Before the conclusion of this chapter on prose literature, one last example from the ancient Tarascans of Michoacán should be cited. As already stated, the *Relación de Michoacán* was set down in writing by order of Viceroy Mendoza around the year 1538 or 1539, at which time the anonymous friar who compiled it explicitly noted that he served only as interpreter and always kept in mind that the elders were the ones who were telling the story. Scholars who have studied this chronicle affirm that there is no doubt that it contains ancient indigenous texts translated into sixteenth-century Spanish. A reading of the fragment offered here will confirm this opinion. This passage tells how young people who fell in love arranged their marriage:

If a young man was attracted to a young girl who had a father, the young people talked it over and he had relations with her. Afterwards he sent one of his relatives or some woman to ask in marriage for her whom he had already known. The father and mother, shocked by this, would ask their daughter whether she had known this young man, and she would say she had not known him. The father of the girl then said: "If this one who is attracted to you has some goods, then he should marry you and plant a piece of land so as to give you something to eat, cultivating it, and he should take care of me when I am old." That is to say, if the father had some employment or property which, because of age, he could not attend,

[11] Anne Dyck (ed.), *Mixteco Texts*, 3–5.

then the son-in-law who asked for his daughter as wife should take care of the work, do it for him. So the father said they should wait a few days, that he should send again. If the daughter did not know the young man who said he had relations with her, then the father took a stick and beat the one who came with the message, because she has said something about his daughter; and thus the young man had to send three or four times in this way in order to marry this young woman.

Then the parents believed that he had known her, and they scolded their daughter for what she had done, saying to her: "I who am your father did not act the way you have acted; you have brought me great dishonor, even casting earth in my eyes"; that is to say, the father would not dare to go before the people or to raise his eyes to look at them because all would look at him and insult him to his face for what she had done. He said more to his daughter: "I, when a young man, married your mother and we had a house; they gave me a dowry of maize and clothes, and they gave me a house; whom do you resemble in this which you have done? Why do you like this dissolute one? Because he was dissolute, he had relations with you to dishonor you." And the mother also scolded her. Then they went to the house of he who had seduced her and took from him everything he had in his house, clothes and grinding stones and the seeds he had prepared for himself, and they insulted him. And if they decided to give her to him, the parents talked to each other saying: "What do we want for our daughter? We cannot make her again a virgin. She is already soiled, for their hearts have undergone a change and have spoken to each other." Then they would bring her to him at his house, the parents accompanying her, and they would give her to him, making clear their reasons. If they were of the same ward, they were married; if not, they did not give her.[12]

Certainly the examples presented show only a very small part of the richness of prose texts in ancient Mexico. Those in Náhuatl deserve special attention, for they hold the key to a deeper understanding of such important pre-Columbian institutions as education, trade, laws, religious fiestas and ceremonies, war, and the daily life of the people. A great number of documents are still waiting for the researcher who will set out to study the soul of Mexico's ancient cultures.

[12] *Relación de Michoacán,* 215–16.

VII

Native Chronicles of the Conquest

THE NAHUAS AND THE MAYAS, equally concerned with the memory of their past, have each left their own accounts of what was the most important and tragic event in their history: the Conquest by foreigners which destroyed forever their ancient ways of life. These chronicles, written in the form and vigorous style of their ancient literature, show the drama of the Conquest as viewed from the side of the conquered. The *Cartas* of Hernán Cortés to the Emperor Charles V are well known, as are the *Historia verdadera de la conquista de la Nueva España* written by Bernal Díaz del Castillo and shorter accounts by other conquistadors. But the testimony of the native wise men has received little attention.

Fray Toribio de Benavente, the famous Motolinía who arrived in Mexico around 1524, understood fully the intense interest which the few surviving historians had in their memories of this event:

> These native Indians recorded carefully, in their year counts, the year in which the Spaniards arrived and entered their land as a very notable thing, which at first frightened them and made them marvel. To see people come over the water (which they had neither seen nor heard could be done), with such strange dress, so audacious, so courageous, so few, and to enter into all the provinces of this land with such authority and boldness as if all the natives were their vassals. Likewise they accepted as a wonder and were terrified by the horses and what the Spaniards could do riding them.... They called the Spaniards *teteuh*, which means gods, and the Spaniards corrupted the word to *teules*....[1]

[1] Fray Toribio de Benavente (Motolinía), *Historia de los Indios de la Nueva España*, 161–62.

There are over a dozen accounts preserved from the Náhuatl world which give the indigenous image of what happened at that time. There are also several native chronicles covering the conquest of Yucatán, including the version of the Chontals of Tabasco and others which describe how the Quichés and Cakchiquels of Guatemala were subjugated.

While these chronicles are valuable historical documents, they are even more valuable for their intensely human literary expression. It is no exaggeration to say that the dramatic force in some of these accounts is comparable only to that of the great classical epics. Whereas Homer in the *Iliad* recalled so vividly many tragic scenes during the fall of Troy, the native writers, who witnessed the struggle and the humiliation, also knew how to bring out the most dramatic moments of the Conquest and the events which followed it. These texts which reflect "the vision of the conquered" are the last and most tragic expression of a culture, as seen at the very moment of its collapse.

This chapter offers a few selections from these native accounts—accompanied by explanations of their origins—which follow the events chronologically. First are some texts left in Náhuatl by Aztec and Tezcocan historians, followed by the testimonies of the Mayas of Yucatán, the Chontals of Tabasco, and the Quichés and Cakchiquels of Guatemala.

The most ancient testimonies about the Conquest in the Náhuatl language seem to have found expression in songs, composed in the ancient style by surviving poets. Two of these poems are examples of the famous *icnocuícatl*, the elegies or sad songs of the Aztec world. The first tells how the Mexican people perished. It shows clearly how deeply the native soul was wounded by the experience of the Conquest.

And all this happened to us.
We saw it,
we marveled at it.
With this sad and mournful destiny
we saw ourselves afflicted.
On the roads lie broken arrows,
our hair is in disarray.
Without roofs are the houses,
and red are their walls with blood.

Worms multiply in the streets and squares,
and on the walls brains are spattered.
Red are the waters, as if they were dyed,
and when we drink,
it seems water of saltpeter.
We have struggled against the walls of adobe,
but our heritage was a net made of holes.
Our shields were our protection
but not even with shields could we defend ourselves.
We have eaten branches of linnet,
we have chewed upon salty witch grass,
bits of adobe and ground earth,
small lizards, rats, worms. . . .
We ate meat
when it was scarcely on the fire.
When the meat was cooked,
we snatched it out of
the very coals and ate it.
They put a price on us.
The price for a young person, for a priest,
a child or a young girl.
And it was enough: for a common man
the price was only two handfuls of corn
or ten portions of caked mosquitoes,
our price was only
twenty portions of salty witch grass.
Gold, jade, rich mantles,
plumage of quetzal,
all that has value
was then counted as nothing. . . .[2]

Another account of how the Mexicans were defeated is in the following poem which tells of Cuauhtémoc being taken prisoner and of the fate of the native princess, Doña Isabel de Moctezuma:

The Mexican is surrounded by war;
the Tlatelolcan is surrounded by war!

[2] MSS *Anónimo de Tlatelolco*, in Mengin (ed.), *Corpus Codicum Americanorum Medii Aevi*, I, fol. 33.

All is blackened by fire, the shooting blazes forth:
now the confusion has spread.
Now they have taken prisoner Cuauhtémoc;
the Mexican princes stretch out their arms to him!
The Mexican is surrounded by war;
the Tlatelolcan is surrounded by war!
Nine days ago amidst tumult they were taken to Coyohuacan;
Cuauhtémoc, Coanácoch, Tetlepanquetzaltzin,
prisoners are the kings.
Tlacotzin comforted them, said to them:
"Oh my nephews, have courage; with chains of gold
are the kings bound, imprisoned."
But Cuauhtémoc, the king, replied:
"Oh my nephew, you are prisoner, you are weighed down with iron."

"Who are you, that you sit next to the Captain General?
Ah, it is Doña Isabel, my little niece!
Then truly the kings are prisoners!
Now certainly you will be a slave, the property of another;
a chain will be forged, quetzal will be woven in Coyohuacan.
Who are you, that you sit next to the Captain General?
Ah, it is Doña Isabel, my little niece!
Then truly the kings are prisoners!"[3]

In addition to these and other songs, there are also the historical accounts written as early as 1528. Especially important is a manuscript in the National Library of Paris, entitled *Unos Anales Históricos de la Nación Mexicana*, set down in Náhuatl anonymously by Tlatelolcans in the above mentioned year. This document brings to light a rather extraordinary fact: there already were some natives who knew the Latin alphabet and used it to put down in writing their remembrances of the past, especially their viewpoint of the Conquest.

Another account in Náhuatl is offered by various native students who, under the direction of Fray Bernardino de Sahagún, rescued the memories recounted by old men who had witnessed the Conquest. The first copy of this text was finished around 1555. Sahagún himself summarizes it in his

---

[3] *Cantares Mexicanos*, fol. 55 v.–r.

Historia. Later on, around 1585, the Náhuatl testimony was revised and included in what is known as the *Códice Florentino.* The account begins by describing the various omens which were seen "when the men of Castile had not yet come to this land," then gives a picture of the most significant happenings during the Conquest, and ends with a discourse "in which Don Hernán Cortés warns all the lords of Mexico, Tezcoco, and Tlacopan" that they must give him their gold and their treasures.

Other native accounts of the Conquest are included in the *Códice Aubin* and in the works of native and mestizo historians such as Tezozómoc, Chimalpain, and Ixtlilxóchitl. Finally, some of the principal pictorial testimonies on the same theme should be mentioned. These are found in the *Códice Florentino* and in the *Lienzo de Tlaxcala,* which dates from the middle of the sixteenth century and is made up of eighty painted squares giving the account of the Tlaxcalans, the Indian allies of the conquistadors. Other native drawings about the Conquest are found in the *Códice Aubin,* in the *Códice Ramírez,* and in the *Historia de las Indias* by Fray Diego de Durán.

The purpose in presenting a translation of several of these texts is not only to show their literary value but also the way in which the ancient Mexicans interpreted the Conquest. According to them, ten years before the arrival of the Spaniards there began a series of ominous occurrences, some of which the natives themselves said they had seen and some others which were said to have happened to Motecuhzoma. Here is the Náhuatl account:

> The first sinister omen: ten years before the men of Castile came for the first time, there was a sinister omen in the sky. Something like a stalk of fire, something like a tongue of fire, like the dawn, it looked as if it was falling bit by bit, as if the sky was wounded. Wide at the bottom, narrow at the top, right in the middle of the sky, right in the center of the heavens it came; right in the heavens it was fixed.
> And this way it was seen: there in the east it showed itself; it was the same at midnight. It was manifest; it continued even at daybreak, until the sun made it disappear. And the time during which it appeared, when it showed itself, was one year. It began in the year 12-House. When it

showed itself, there was a great clamor; the people clapped their hands over their mouths; they were terrified; they talked about it constantly.

The second sinister omen which happened here in Mexico: the temple of Huitzilopochtli took fire by itself; it was surrounded with flames; it seemed that no one set fire to it, but it burned by itself. This was the divine place, the place called Tlacateccan (House of Command).

It was seen how the columns burned. From the inside came the flames of fire, the tongues of fire, the flashes of fire.

Very quickly the fire destroyed the wooden part of the temple. Immediately there was a noisy shouting; they said: "Mexicans, come quickly; we will put it out! Bring your water jars. . . ." But when they threw water on it, when they tried to put it out, it burned with even more flames. They could not put it out; it all burned. . . .

The seventh sinister omen: many times something was caught, something was trapped in the nets. Those who worked in the water caught a kind of ash-colored bird, like a crane. At last they took it and showed it to Motecuhzoma in the Black House (House of Magic).

The sun had arrived at the zenith; it was midday. There was a kind of mirror on the top of the bird's head, like the wheel of a spindle, in reverse spiral; it was as if it had been perforated down through the middle. And there in the mirror was seen the sky and the stars. . . . And Motecuhzoma took it as a very evil omen.

But when he looked a second time at the top of the bird's head, he saw there, in the distance, people moving quickly, very haughty, striking out rudely. Some were making war on others, and they were carried on the backs of something like deer.

Immediately he called his magicians, his wise men. He said to them: "Do you understand what I have seen? Some kind of people, erect and very agitated! . . ."

And they, wishing to answer, came to look; everything had disappeared, they saw nothing.[4]

Motecuhzoma, disturbed by these and other omens, called the wise men and wizards to inquire the meaning of what he considered evil predictions. The wizards could give no answer. But a country man who had

[4] *Códice Florentino*, Book XII, Chapter I. Most of the Book XII of this codex has been published in León-Portilla (ed.), *The Broken Spears.*

come from the Gulf Coast brought news which increased their amazement and caused great alarm. Along the coast had been seen "something like towers or little hills which came floating on top of the sea." Strange people came, "of very white skin, whiter than ours, and they all had long beards and their hair grew down to their ears. . . ." This news awakened dread in Motecuhzoma, who decided to send messengers; he believed that possibly Quetzalcóatl and other gods had returned in accordance with predictions in their books of pictures. Here is the account taken from the indigenous text in the *Códice Florentino*:

It was as if he thought that the newly arrived one was our prince Quetzalcóatl.

Thus it seemed in his heart; for this one had come by himself, he had come from there [the east]; he came to know the place of his throne, of his dignity. As if for this he had gone, only to return.

Motecuhzoma sent out five emissaries who went to meet him and to present gifts. A priest led them, he who had in his charge and under his name the sanctuary of Yohualichan.

The second was one from Tepoztlan; the third was from Tizatlan; the fourth from Huehuetlan; and the fifth from Mictlan.

He said to them:

"Come here, tiger knights, come here. It is said that once more our lord has arrived at our land. Go to meet him, go to hear what he says; listen well to what he tells you. Listen well that you should remember. I have here what you must take to our lord:

This is the treasure of Quetzalcóatl: a serpent mask made of turquoise.

A crosspiece for the chest, made of quetzal plumes.

A necklace woven in the manner of a mat; in the middle of this is a gold disc.

And a shield with crossbands of gold and even with mother-of-pearl; it has quetzal plumes around the edge and some streamers of the same plumage.

Also a mirror such as those fastened on the backs of dancers, decorated with quetzal feathers. This mirror looks like a shield of turquoise; it is turquoise mosaic, it is incrusted with turquoise, adorned with turquoise.

And an anklet of *chachihuites*, with little gold bells.

Also a dart-thrower adorned with turquoise, all covered with turquoise.
It is as if it had little serpent heads; it has serpent heads.
And some obsidian sandals. . . ."[5]

The messengers arrived at the Gulf where they found the supposed
Quetzalcóatl, that is, Hernán Cortés, and the other Spaniards. Following
Motecuhzoma's instructions, they spoke with those they thought to be
the gods who had returned from across the great water. They were able
to speak with them through the princess Malinche, who had been presented to Cortés as a gift and who knew Náhuatl and Maya, and also
Jerónimo de Aguilar, a Spaniard who could translate from Maya to
Castilian. When they returned to Mexico-Tenochtitlan, the messengers
told Motecuhzoma about everything they had seen:

> This being done, they informed Motecuhzoma. They told him how they
> had gone to observe and what they had seen and what was the food of
> these people.
> And when he heard what those who were sent had to communicate, he
> was amazed and struck with wonder. And their kind of nourishment
> astonished him greatly.
> Also it caused him great wonder to hear how the cannon fires, how the
> noise resounds, and how because of this a person can faint, how this con-
> fuses a person's ears. And how, when the shot falls, something like a stone
> comes out from its inside, how it rains fire, sparks fall; and the smoke
> which comes from it, this is very noxious, it smells like putrid mud, it
> enters the head and is very disturbing.
> Then if it strikes against a hill, as it did, it breaks a hole, it splits the hill
> open; and if it strikes against a tree, it breaks that into splinters as if it
> was a portent, as if someone had blown from the inside.
> Their war equipment is all of iron. Their dress is iron, something like
> a helmet of iron they put on their heads, their swords are iron, their arrows,
> their shields; iron are their spears.
> They are carried on the backs of their "deer." These are as high as
> the roofs.
> All parts of the bodies of the men of Castile are covered, only their faces
> appear. They are white, as if they were made of lime. They have yellow

[5] *Ibid.*, Book XII, Chapter III.

hair but some have black. Long are their beards, also yellow; and their mustaches are yellow. Their hair is fine and curly, a little wavy.

As for their food, it is human nourishment. They eat much; it is white, not heavy, as if it were straw, wood of the maize stalk, and the taste is like the inside of the maize stalk; a little sweet, a little as if it was besmeared with honey. It is eaten like honey, it is sweet food.

Then, their dogs are enormous, with ears hanging down and close to the head, with long tongues hanging out; they have eyes which shoot out fire, throw out sparks; their eyes are yellow, a deep yellow. Their bellies are proud, distended like a ribbed framework. They are very stout and strong; they are not peaceful, they go panting, they go with their tongues hanging out. They are marked the color of tigers, with many colored spots.

When he had heard all this, Motecuhzoma was filled with terror, as if his heart had contracted, as if his heart had swooned; he was overcome with anguish.[6]

After this information from his messengers, Motecuhzoma was even more disturbed. He again sent an embassy with captives to be sacrificed in the presence of those he imagined to be the returned gods. Filled with dread and uncertainty, he thought of retiring to the ancient sanctuaries and waiting there for whatever would happen. He was especially concerned to know if the "gods" (the conquistadors) wanted to meet him:

And when Moctecuhzoma learned that they asked about him, that they were inquiring about his person, that the gods wanted to see his face, then his heart beat fast, he was terrified, he wanted to flee. He wanted to hide himself, he was anxious to hide himself. He wanted to hide from them, he wanted to escape from the gods. He thought and he pondered; he plotted and he schemed; he contrived a plan; he meditated and he continued meditating about going to some remote cave.

And to some of those in whom he had great confidence, whose hearts were trustworthy, he made this known to them. They said to him:

"We know the place of the dead, the House of the Sun, the Land of Tláloc, and the House of Cintli. You would have to go there. To whichever you prefer."

And he had his preference; he preferred to go to the House of Cintli [Temple of the Corn Goddess]. But this he could not do. He could not

6 *Ibid.*, Book XII, Chapter IV.

hide himself, he could not conceal himself. He was no longer confident, he was no longer able to act; he could no longer do anything.

The words with which the magicians had confused his heart, torn his heart, had made him giddy, had left him languid and weak; he remained doubtful and uncertain whether he could hide himself there in the place mentioned.

He did nothing except wait for them. He did nothing except retreat within his heart; he did nothing except resign himself; and at last he mastered his heart, he retreated within himself, he was prepared to watch and marvel at what had to happen.[7]

Meanwhile the Spaniards started to march. At the land of Tlaxcala their first encounter was with a group of Otomís sent out by the Tlaxcalans to fight them. When the Tlaxcalans saw the superiority of the strangers' armament, they astutely decided to become allied with them in order to attack their hated enemies, the Aztecs. This was the real reason the lords of Tlaxcala welcomed the Spaniards:

Then immediately the lords of Tlaxcala went to meet them.

They took with them food: wild chickens, eggs, white tortillas, fine tortillas.

They said:

"You are weary, our lords."

Those replied:

"Where is your house? From where do you come?"

They said:

"We are from Tlaxcala. You are weary; you have arrived and have entered your land; Tlaxcala is your house. The City of the Eagle, Tlaxcala, is your house. . . ."

They led them, they brought them, they showed them the way. They let them stay, they allowed them to enter their great house. They honored them greatly, they supplied all that they needed, they joined with them, and then they gave them their daughters.

Then those asked them:

"Where is Mexico? How far is it?"

They replied:

"It is not very far. You can arrive in three days. It is a fine place. And

[7] *Ibid.*, Book XII, Chapter IX.

[they are] very brave, great warriors, conquerors. On all sides they have conquered."[8]

Now allied with the lords of Tlaxcala, Cortés and his people continued their march. They marched towards Cholula, and, possibly incited by the Tlaxcalans, they carried out a terrible massacre there upon discovering what they considered treachery. Then once more the conquistadors, accompanied by the Tlaxcalans, continued their march towards the Valley of Mexico. New emissaries from Motecuhzoma met them in the vicinity of the volcanoes. The native historians delighted in painting the reaction of the strangers when they received the many presents of gold sent by Motecuhzoma:

And then Motecuhzoma sent, designated some chieftains as envoys; Tzihuacpopocatzin was at the head of these, and there were many others representing him. They went to meet [the Spaniards] near Popocatépetl, near Iztactépetl, there in the Place of the Eagle.

They gave the men of Castile banners of gold, banners of quetzal plumage, and gold necklaces. And when they had given them these, the faces [of the Spaniards] smiled, they were very happy, they were delighted. As if they were monkeys, they lifted up the gold, as if it gave them a great feeling of satisfaction, as if their hearts were revived.

What is certain is that they had a great thirst for that gold. Their bodies took on an air of importance because of it, they had a frantic hunger for it. Like hungry pigs they craved that gold. They snatched up greedily the banners of gold, they swung them from side to side, they examined them from top to bottom. They were like people who speak a barbarous language; everything they said was in a barbarous tongue.[9]

Soon after leaving behind the volcanoes, the Spaniards entered into the Tezcocan domain. Here the prince Ixtlilxóchitl also decided to become allied with them. Finally Hernán Cortés and his men approached the great city of Mexico-Tenochtitlan, walking along the causeway which came from Ixtapalapa on the south. On November 8, 1519, Motecuhzoma and Hernán Cortés met face to face. The Aztec sovereign said these words to the mysterious foreigner:

[8] *Ibid.*, Book XII, Chapter X.
[9] *Ibid.*, Book XII, Chapter XIII.

"My lord, you are weary, you are tired. But now you have come to your land. You have arrived at your city, Mexico. Here you have come to sit upon your throne. Oh, for a brief time they have kept it for you, they preserved it, those who have gone away, those who were taking your place, the kings Itzcoatzin, Motecuhzomatzin the Elder, Axayácac, Tízoc, Ahuítzotl. Oh, for what a brief time did they care for it in your name, did they rule over the city of Mexico. The common people were cared for under their shoulders, under their power.

"Do they see, perhaps know those they left, those who stayed behind? Oh, may one of them be watching and see with amazement what I now see in front of me! What now I see, I the remaining one, the survivor of our lords. No, no I am not dreaming, I did not get up from the ground still sleeping, I do not see it in dreams, I am not dreaming. . . .

"It is indeed you that I have seen, my eyes have rested on your face! For five days, for ten days I have been in agony; my gaze has been fixed on the Region of Mystery. And you have come from among the clouds, from within the mist. Just as it was left recorded by the kings, by those who reigned, those who governed your city, that you would come to install yourself in your place, your seat of honor, that you would come here. . . .

"So now it has happened; now you are here; with great fatigue, with great effort you have come. You have arrived in your land; come now and rest; take possession of your royal houses; refresh your body. Be in your land, my lord!"

When Motecuhzoma's address was finished and the marquis [Cortés] had heard it, Malintzin translated it for him, explained it to him. And when he perceived the meaning of Motecuhzoma's discourse, then he gave his answer through the mouth of Malintzin. He said it in a strange tongue, he said it in a barbaric tongue:

"Be reassured, Motecuhzoma, have no fear. We have great affection for you. Today our hearts are at peace. We see your face, we hear you. For a long time now we have wanted to see you."

And he said more:

"Now we have come, now we have arrived at your house in Mexico; in this way, therefore, you can hear our words now with complete tranquility."

Then those [the Spaniards] who had accompanied him shook his hand.

They patted him on the back, by which they showed their affection for him.[10]

From that moment on, the Spaniards were established in Mexico-Tenochtitlan as guests. Motecuhzoma became practically a prisoner. At about this time Hernán Cortés had to leave the city with part of his men to fight Pánfilo de Narváez who had come by order of Diego Velázquez, governor of Cuba, to take over the command from Cortés. During Cortés' absence, Pedro de Alvarado, or "The Sun," as the Aztecs called him, took advantage of the great fiesta of Tóxcatl, which was being celebrated at that time, to carry out a slaughter in the city. The native text gives a truly dramatic picture, which relates the treachery and crime of Alvarado:

Thus it happened. While they were enjoying the fiesta, while there was dancing, there was singing, already one song was entwined with another and the songs were as the uproar of waves, at this precise moment the men of Castile decided to kill the people. Then they came there, all came armed for war.

They came and closed the exits, the passageways, the entrances: the Eagle Gate to the smaller palace, the Cane Tip Gate, the Serpent of Mirrors Gate from Tezcacóac. And as soon as these were closed, they placed guards there; then no one could go out. With things arranged thus, quickly they entered the Sacred Courtyard to kill the people. They came on foot, carrying their shields of wood or of metal and their swords.

Quickly they came up to those who were dancing; they rushed to the place of the drums; they struck at the one who was playing the drums; they cut off both his arms. Then they chopped off his head and it fell far away.

In a moment they were slashing at them, they were running their spears through the people and hacking them; with the swords they wounded them. Some they attacked from behind and immediately these fell to the ground with their entrails hanging out. Others they severed the head and then chopped it into small pieces.

Others they struck on the shoulders, made gashes in them; their bodies remained mutilated. Some they wounded in the thigh, some in the calf, others straight in the abdomen, and all their entrails fell to the ground.

[10] *Ibid.*, Book XII, Chapter XVI.

There were some who even tried vainly to run away; they went dragging their intestines and their feet became entangled in them. Anxious to save themselves, they found no place to go.

Some tried to get out; there at the entrance they were stabbed, they were cut down. Some scaled the walls; but they could not save themselves. Others went into the communal houses; there they were safe for a while. Others lay among the dead; in order to escape they pretended to be dead. By appearing to be dead, they were safe; but if anyone got up on his feet, they saw it and they cut him down.

The blood of the warriors ran as if it was water, like water which makes little pools; the stench of blood filled the air, and the stench of the entrails which seemed to crawl along by themselves.

And the men of Castile went everywhere, even searching the communal houses; everywhere they thrust their weapons, looking to see if someone was hidden there; everywhere they probed, they pried into everything. They thrust into all parts of the communal houses.[11]

The angry Aztecs then surrounded the conquistadors who had to take refuge in the Palace of Axayácatl. About this time Cortés returned, victorious over Narváez and his men. He first tried to appease the Aztecs, making use of Motecuhzoma, who lost his life in the effort.

A few days later the Spaniards began preparations to abandon Mexico-Tenochtitlan by night. It was then that the Aztec warrtors had their revenge, during what the Spaniards called the "sad night." Native historians described how the conquistadors were blocked as they fled by the Tacuba causeway. The victorious Aztecs then divided the war booty which they recovered from the Spaniards. Cortés' troops had to take refuge with their allies, where they prepared their final attack on the Aztec capital.

In Mexico-Tenochtitlan, Prince Cuitláhuac was elected supreme ruler. His reign lasted only a short time, for he died in the smallpox epidemic which struck the city. The young Cuauhtémoc succeeded him.

A few months later the Spaniards reappeared with thousands of Indian allies, with their brigantines, their cannons, and their pack horses, and at last took possession of the great capital. There are many texts in the

[11] *Ibid.*, Book XII, Chapter XX.

native sources describing the battles, the struggle, and the hunger during the siege of Mexico, which lasted for eighty days. Náhuatl and Spanish chroniclers alike give ample testimony to the fact that there were heroic deeds on both sides. Finally the city fell on the day 1-Serpent of the year 3-House, or the thirteenth of August, 1521. The text transcribed here paints in vivid colors the tragedy of the Aztec collapse:

> Then once again the men of Castile killed the people; many died on that occasion. But the flight had already begun with which the war would end. Some were shouting, they said:
>
> "It is enough! ... Let us escape! At least we can eat herbs!"
>
> And when the others heard this, then the general flight began. Some went by water, others went by the main causeway. Even there some were killed; they [the Spaniards] were angry because some still carried their bludgeons and their shields.
>
> Those who lived in the city houses went in the direction of Amáxac, straight towards the place where the roads divide. There the frightened people separated. Some went towards Tepeyácac, some went towards Xoxohuiltitlan, some went towards Nonohualco. None went towards Xóloc or Mazatzintamalco, none went there.
>
> But all those who lived on boats and those who lived on the wooden rafts fixed in the lake and the inhabitants of Tolmayecan went only by water. And some went in water up to their chests and others in water up to their necks. And some even drowned in the deep water. They carried the very young children on their shoulders. There was howling everywhere. But some little children were happy; it amused them to ride along holding on with their arms and legs.
>
> Those who owned boats, those who had boats, left at night; but a few left in the daytime. They almost ran into each other as they went along.
>
> For their part, the men of Castile were searching the people along the roads. They were looking for gold. Jade, quetzal plumage, and turquoise had no importance for them.
>
> Women carried it in their breasts, under their petticoats, and the men, we carried it in our mouths or in our *maxtli* [the cloth which covers the private parts].
>
> And also they took possession, they selected among the women, the white ones, those with dark skins, those with dark-skinned bodies. And some

163

women during the plunder covered their faces with mud and put on ragged clothes, tattered underskirts, tattered blouses. Everything which they wore was in shreds.

Also, some men were taken captive, the brave and strong, those who had stout hearts, and also young boys to be their servants. And some of these they branded with hot irons close to the mouth; some on the cheeks, some on the lips.

When our defense was laid down, the time when we were defeated, it was the year sign 3-House, the day on the magical calendar 1-Serpent.

After Cuauhtémoc was taken prisoner, they took him to Acachinanco at night. But the next day, when the sun had risen a little, many men of Castile came back again. It was their last time. They came in battle dress, with coats of mail and metal helmets, but no one with a sword, no one with a shield.

All covered their noses with white handkerchiefs; they were nauseated by the dead bodies, already disintegrating, the bodies already become putrid. And all came on foot.

They came, dragging by their mantles Cuauhtémoc and Conacotzin and Tetlepanquetzaltzin. The three came in a line. . . .[12]

The fragments cited are only a small part of the abundant testimonies left by Náhuatl wise men concerning the destruction of their city and the loss of everything they had. In these masterpieces of native literature can be found a key to the understanding of what has been called "the trauma of the Conquest." But for the Spaniards the conquest of Mexico-Tenochtitlan was not the end. Captains and soldiers marched to distant parts of the country. The Tlaxcalans and other conquered natives continued serving as auxiliary troops. Among the innumerable peoples who were conquered were various Maya groups who also left their own accounts of the Conquest.

Preserved in the *Chilam Balam of Chumayel* is a section which could well be called the *ḳah-lay* or "account of the Conquest." In the form of an epic poem with occasional lyric passages, it tells of the disgrace of the Mayas of Yucatán, who also gave way before the onslaught of the Spaniards. The manner of expression used in this text, translated from Maya,

[12] *Ibid.*, Book XII, Chapter XXXIX.

164

recalls in some ways the Hebrew prophecies and also the sad songs or *icnocuícatl* of the Náhuatl world. The *chilam* priest in this manner told about the white men, *dzules*, foreigners, the "eaters of custard apples":

> Recollections of the *katúns* and of the years in which for the first time the land of Yucatán was conquered by the *dzules*, the foreigners, the white men. It was within the 11-Ahau Katún that they seized the Water Gate, the port of Ecab. They came from the east. When they arrived, they say that their first food was custard apples. This is the reason why they called them "the strangers who eat custard apples." "Foreign lords who munch upon custard apples" was their name. Nacom Balum, this is the householder, was made prisoner when they seized the port of Ecab. He was made captive by the first Spanish captain Juan [Francisco] de Montejo, the first conquistador. In this same *katún* it happened that they arrived at Ichcaansihó.[13]

Later on, comparing the ancient way of life, when "the lords of the birds, of the precious stones, of the carved stones, and of the tigers" still guided and protected the Mayas, with the changes brought by the conquistadors, the *Chilam Balam of Chumayel* laments in this fashion:

> They did not wish to join with the foreigners, nor did they desire Christianity. They did not know that they would have to pay tribute. The lords of the birds, the lords of the precious stones, the lords of the carved stones, the lords of the tigers had always guided them and protected them. One thousand six hundred years and three hundred years more and then their life had to come to an end! For they had always known within themselves the length of their days.
>
> The moon, the year, the day and the night, the breath of life were fulfilled and they passed. The blood was fulfilled and came to the place of its rest, as also it had come to its power and its dignity. During their time they had repeated the good prayers; they had sought the lucky days when the good stars watched over them. Then they kept vigil, when the good stars watched over them. Then all was good.
>
> In them there was wisdom. Then was no sin. In them there was holy devotion. Life was wholesome. There was no sickness then; there was no aching of the bones; there was no fever for them; there was no smallpox;

---

[13] Roys, *Chilam Balam of Chumayel*, 80–81. Maya text, 21.

there was no burning in the chest; there was no pain in the stomach; there was no consumption. Raised up straight was the body then. It was not thus the foreigners did after they came here. They brought shameful things when they came. Everything was lost in carnal sin. No more lucky days were granted us. This was the cause of our sickness.[14]

Along with expressions of deeply lyric feeling, such as those cited, are also found factual accounts describing the arrival of the Spaniards in Yucatán. From the various chronicles written by survivors of the Conquest, there is preserved, among others, that of the chief Ah Nakuk Pech, lord of Chac-Kulub-Chen. In his writing he tells of the several raids by the Spaniards along the coast of Yucatán beginning in the year 1511. He mentions the coming of Jerónimo de Aguilar, as well as the passage of Hernán Cortés through Cozumel early in 1519. And at the end he gives his attention to the final phase of the conquest of Yucatán, which was carried out from the west around 1540. As in the *Chilam Balam of Chumayel*, he also refers to the Spaniards in this chronicle by the name of "eaters of custard apples," explaining that this fruit was not eaten before they came. Transcribed here is Ah Nakuk Pech's account of what happened between the years 1542 and 1544:

The year 1542 was when the men of Castile settled down in the land of Ichcaansihó. . . . It was then that tribulations came and entered there for the first time, when, it is known, the men of Castile came for the third time to this land and established themselves forever, that is to say, they settled down. The first time when they came to Chichén Itzá, then was when they ate custard apples for the first; since no one ate these custard apples, when they ate them, they were called "eaters of custard apples." The second time they came to Chichén Itzá was when they overthrew Nacón Cupul. The third time they came was when they established themselves forever, and that, it is known, was in the year 1542, the year in which they settled down forever here in the land of Ichcaansihó. It was the 13-Kan, the year-bearer, according to Maya count.

The year 1543 was the year in which the men of Castile were in the north, near the land of the Cheeles, looking for Maya men to be slaves, because there were no men slaves in T-Hó. They came suddenly, looking

14 *Ibid.*, 83. Maya text, 22.

and searching for men slaves. When they came to Popoce, after having left T-Hó, they imposed heavy tribute there in Popoce. And then they left and came to Tikom for many days; and after they arrived in Tikom, it is known, it was twenty days before the men of Castile left there.

It was in 1544, it is known, the year in which Cauacán was given over to the foreign lord, the captain Asiesa. In Cauacán the lords were gathered together and as tribute they gave honey, wild turkeys, and maize. It was in Cauacán, later on, that they shut up in prison the counselor Caamal of Sisal and demanded tribute and the records from all the villages. . . .[15]

The very style of this narration is reminiscent of other purely pre-Hispanic chronicles. It shows the Maya interest not only in preserving the remembrance of the past but also in setting it down with the proper notations of time. There is, in the Chontal Maya tongue of Tabasco, a text which also refers to episodes related to the Conquest, including the arrival of Hernán Cortés in 1525 in Acalan on the Gulf Coast during his expedition to the Hibueras in what is today Honduras. The most interesting section of this account is the mention of proposals made to the Chontal chieftain by Cuauhtémoc, who accompanied Cortés as prisoner. According to the Chontal version, Cuauhtémoc urged the lord Pax-bolonachá, the chief of this region, not to allow Cortés to subjugate them, but to fight in defense of his people and their ancient ways of life. The Chontal chieftain, fearing the strength of the Spaniards, informed Cortés about this, which cost Cuauhtémoc his life.

Since this document is one of the very few preserved in the Chontal tongue of Tabasco and because it contains this little-known version about the cause of Cuauhtémoc's death, the central portion of it is presented here:

The Spaniards came to this land in the year 1525. The captain was called Don Martín [Hernán] Cortés. They came in from Tanocic and passed through the village of Taxich where the Xacchute land begins. They took provisions in the village of Tazahhaa. And being there with all his people, he [Cortés] sent to call Paxbolonachá who was, as we have already said, the king; this one brought together all the leaders from all his villages,

---

[15] *Crónica de Chac-Xulub-Chen,* in Agustín Yáñez (ed.), *Crónicas de la Conquista,* 190–92.

from the village of Taxunum and the leaders from the village of Chabte and the leaders from the village of Atapan and the leaders from the village of Tatzanto, because he was not able to do anything without consulting these leaders. He told them what the thing was about. . . . And they said it was not right that their king should be called by the Spaniards because they did not know what they wanted.

Then one of the leaders, called Chocpaloquem, stood up and said: "Oh King and Lord, you remain in your domain and your city; I would go and see what the Spaniards want." And thus he went, in the name of the king, with other leaders who were called Pazinchiquigua and Paxguaapuc and Paxchagchan, companions from Paloquem. And coming into the presence of the Captain del Valle [Cortés] and of the Spaniards, those did not believe them; they must have had among them the one who told them that the king who was summoned would not come. And thus the captain said to them: "The king must come, for I wish to see him; for I do not come for war nor to do evil; for I only wish to pass through to see the land, whatever there is to see; for I will do him much good if he receives me well."

And having understood this, those who came in the name of the king went back and told Paxbolonachá, their king, who was waiting in the village. And after they had returned, all the chiefs came together, and the king said to them: "I wish to go myself to see the captain and the Spaniards, for I wish to see them and to know what they want and why they have come." And thus Paxbolonachá went.

The Spaniards, knowing this, went out to receive him, and the Captain del Valle with them. And the Chontals had brought many presents for them: honey, wild chickens, maize, copal, and much fruit. And the captain said: "King Paxbolonachá, I have come here to your land, for I am sent by the lord of the world, the emperor, who is on his throne in Spain, who sent me to see the land and what kind of people populate it; for I do not come for war, but only to ask you to show me the way to Ulúa, which is also Mexico, the land where one finds silver and plumage and cocoa; all this I would see as I pass through." And thus Paxbolonachá replied to him that he would let him pass in good time and that he should go with him to his place and his land and that there they would discuss whatever was necessary. And the captain replied to him that he should be at ease, that indeed he would go. And so they were resting there for twenty days.

And there was Cuauhtémoc, king of Mexico, who came with the captain Cortés, and Cuauhtémoc spoke secretly with Paxbolonachá, the king: "Oh King, there will come a time when these Spaniards will give us much trouble and do us much harm and they will kill our people. To me it seems that we should kill them, since I bring many people and you are many." And this said Cuauhtémoc to Paxbolonachá, king of the Chontals. Having heard this reason, Poxbolonachá replied: "I will see about this. Leave it for now, that we may consider it." And thinking about the matter, he saw the Spaniards had done nothing evil, they had not beaten nor killed any Indian, and they only asked for honey, chickens, and maize and some fruits, which they gave them each day; and since they had done them no harm, he could not have two faces toward them nor be of two hearts towards the Spaniards. And Cuauhtémoc was constantly molesting him because he wanted to kill all the Spaniards; and seeing that he was molested, Paxbolonachá went to the Captain del Valle and said to him: "Captain del Valle, this leader and captain of the Mexicans you have brought, treat him with care, that he should not be treacherous with you, because three or four times he has suggested to me that we kill you." Having heard this, the Captain del Valle took Cuauhtémoc and threw him in prison, and the third day that he was prisoner they took him out and baptized him, and it is not verified whether they gave him the name Don Juan or Don Fernando; and having finished baptizing him, they cut off his head and it was nailed to a silk cotton tree in front of the house of the gods in the village of Yaxzam. . . .[16]

A last example from the Maya texts about the Conquest is taken from the *Memorial de Tecpan-Atitlán*, also known as *Annals of the Cakchiquels*. It contains the story of the wanderings of those groups which settled in Guatemala and most of their adventures, including events which took place during the sixteenth century. This text is better understood by remembering that the conquest of this part of the Maya world began early in 1524, when Cortés sent the *adelantado*, Don Pedro de Alvarado, Tunatiuh, to subject the natives of this southern region. The first encounters were with the Quichés, neighbors of the Cakchiquels. The Quichés were first conquered at the end of February in 1524.

---

[16] This text has been published by France V. Scholes and Ralph L. Roys in *The Maya Chontal Indians of Acalan-Tixchel*, 271–72.

On the day 1-Ganel [February 20, 1524] the Quichés were destroyed by the men of Castile. Their chief, called Tunatiuh Adelantado, conquered all the villages. Until that time their faces were not known. Until a short time before wood and stone had been worshiped.

Having arrived at Xelahub, there they overcame the Quichés; all the Quichés who came out to meet the men of Castile were reduced to nothing. The Quichés were destroyed there in front of Xelahub.

Then they [the Spaniards] left for the city of Gumarcaah where they were received by the Quiché kings, by Ahpop and by Ahpop Qamahay, who paid them tribute. But soon the lords were tortured by Tunatiuh [Pedro de Alvarado]. On the day 4-Qat [March 7, 1524], Kings Ahpop and Ahpop Qamahay were burned by Tunatiuh. The heart of Tunatiuh had no pity for people during the war. . . .[17]

After the fall of the Quichés, the ferocious Tunatiuh [Alvarado] continued to extend his conquest. In the beginning he had an alliance with the Cakchiquels, long-time enemies of the Quichés; for, like Hernán Cortés in his conquest of Mexico, Alvarado took advantage of already existing rivalries among the various native kingdoms. In this way, assisted by the Cakchiquels, he was able to conquer quickly and easily other peoples such as the Zutujils and even those of Cuzcatlán in what is today the Republic of El Salvador.

However, this alliance with the Cakchiquels ended because of the conqueror's greed. Aroused by a sorcerer, the Cakchiquels left their capital city and began to carry out acts of hostility against the foreigners. The native historian, who points out precisely the dates on which various events occurred, shows a clear intention of transmitting his remembrances to those who would come after him. Because of this intention, the exclamation "Oh my children!" often appears in the text. The following is the pathetic account of men who knew how to cherish the memory of their ancient greatness and also record their recent disgrace:

Then Tunatiuh [Alvarado] asked the kings for gold. He wanted them to give him a great quantity of metal, their vessels and their diadems. And since they did not bring it all immediately, Tunatiuh became angry with the kings and said to them: "Why have you not brought me the metal?

[17] *Anales de los Cakchiqueles*, 124–25.

If you do not bring me all the gold of the tribes, I will burn you and I will hang you," he said to the lords.

Then Tunatiuh sentenced them to pay one thousand two hundred gold pesos. The kings tried to have this reduced; they began to weep, but Tunatiuh did not consent and he said to them:

"Procure the metal and bring it within five days. Alas for you, if you do not bring it! This is my will!" Thus he said to the lords.

They had already brought half the gold to Tunatiuh when a man appeared, an emissary of the gods, who said to the kings: "I am the ray of light. I will kill the men of Castile; they shall perish by fire. When I cause the beat of the drum, all shall come out from the city; the lords shall go to the other side of the river. This I will do on the day 7-Ahmak [August 26, 1524]." Thus spoke that sorcerer to the lords. And actually the lords believed that they should respect the orders of that man. Half the gold had already been given when we made our escape.

The day 7-Ahmak we carried out our flight. We abandoned the city of Iximché then because of the sorcerer. Afterwards the kings left. "Certainly Tunatiuh will die in a moment," they said. "There is no more war in the heart of Tunatiuh; he is satisfied now with the metal which has been given him."

This was the way in which we abandoned the city on the day 7-Ahmak because of the sorcerer, oh my children!

But Tunatiuh knew what the kings had done. Ten days after we fled from the city, Tunatiuh began to make war on us. The day 4-Camey [September 5, 1524] they began to make us suffer. We dispersed under the trees, under the liana, oh my children! All our tribes began fighting with Tunatiuh. Then the men of Castile began to march, they went out of the city, leaving it deserted.

Then the Cakchiquels began to harass the foreigners. We opened up deep pits and holes to trap the horses and planted sharp sticks so they would be killed. At the same time the people made war on them. Many men of Castile perished and the horses died in the horse traps. . . .[18]

The downfall of the Cakchiquel nation and its submission is summarized dramatically in the following words:

Tribute in gold was paid to Tunatiuh; we paid tribute of four hundred

18 *Ibid.*, 128–30.

men and four hundred women to work in Pangán, under orders from Tunatiuh, to construct the City of the Lord. All this, all, we ourselves saw it, oh my children![19]

The Cakchiquel sages who saw all this with their own eyes were the same who saved from oblivion this "vision of the conquered" and wrote it down for their children and descendants. As in the case of Aztec and other native accounts of the Conquest, this is one of the most dramatic examples of indigenous historical prose telling about the ruin of a people who had known what it was to be great. Perhaps we can take these as the final words of the wise men who were the last participants of a civilization, the remnants of which even today are a source of amazement to anyone who seeks to understand human experience, art, feelings, and thought as they existed in the isolated context of ancient America.

It would be far from true to give the impression that during colonial years and even up to the present, native men no longer composed songs, poems, and other literary productions. But these later works remain outside the scope of this study, which is limited to pre-Hispanic creations and to those contemporary with the Conquest. Colonial and modern indigenous literatures must be considered separately, and there is enough material to fill many books on the subject. These later works of the descendants of the artists of flower-and-song undoubtedly reflect something of the trauma of the Conquest. But above all they show the new life which resulted from a fusion of cultures, a mingling of feelings, and a combination of ancient and modern ideas.

[19] *Ibid.*, 133–34.

Conclusion

THE LITERARY PRODUCTION of ancient Mexico was far more prolific than is generally recognized. Although there were tremendous losses during the Conquest and the upheaval which followed, many texts are still preserved, and an immense field for research is open to anyone possessing literary sensitivity and a knowledge of the indigenous languages.

As already shown in the present work, indigenous poetry and prose take various forms. There are the great epic poems recalling cosmological myths and legends about the gods and culture heroes; there are the sacred hymns and an extraordinary variety of religious poetry which is often lyrical and sometimes dramatic; there still remain chronicles and historical accounts based on the ancient annals; and there are stories born of creative imagination and instructive texts covering different subjects, among which the talks of the elders are noteworthy.

No doubt the greatest wealth of literary texts has come down to us from the Nahuas of Central Mexico, and it is no exaggeration to say that there are thousands of folios in the Náhuatl tongue in the libraries and archives of Mexico, the United States, and the Old World. There are also manuscripts preserved from the various Maya groups; some of these have already been translated into European languages, and others are waiting to have their contents made known. The examples quoted in this work have shown the literary value, the art which is inherent in many compositions of the pre-Columbian world. If very little remains from other cultures such as the Mixtec, Zapotec, Otomí, and Tarascan, at least it is sufficient to give us a clue to their forms of expression and the procedures they used.

The reason more literary texts have been preserved from one particular culture is probably directly related to the presence of outstanding friars and some native survivors who undertook to save from oblivion what they considered to be a significant heritage. In this connection we owe a debt of gratitude to the great Bernardino de Sahagún for his humanistic approach and his almost modern methods of scientific research.

In regard to the origin of the texts, already discussed in the Introduction, the reader has probably looked for the names of the wise men, historians, and poets who were the authors of the various compositions. In some cases these names were given—for example, Tecayehuatzin of Huexotzinco, Ayocuan of Tecamachalco, Nezahualcóyotl and Nezahualpilli of Tezcoco.[1] It must be emphasized, however, that many texts cannot and should not be attributed to specific persons. As in other cultures, here also the ancient myths, the sacred hymns, and the instructive discourses were the work of groups of learned men and priests who, through the centuries, preserved and enriched the literary legacy. Since they express the highest ideals of a people, they often provide a key to the understanding of the art, the traditional institutions, and, indeed, the ancient culture as a whole. There is, for instance, a reference to their ideals in the field of artistic creation in the following text which describes the artist. He who creates something is given the title of Toltec:

The artist: a Toltec, disciple, resourceful, diverse, restless.
The true artist, capable, well trained, expert;
he converses with his heart, finds things with his mind.
The true artist draws from his heart; he works with delight;
does things calmly, with feeling; works like a Toltec;
invents things, works skillfully, creates; he arranges things;
adorns them; reconciles them.[2]

This ideal of the true artist survives even today in the souls of many natives. Four centuries after the Conquest there are still potters, weavers, featherwork artists, singers and dancers, men who converse with their hearts, who work with delight and do things calmly. In spite of poverty

[1] See León-Portilla, *Trece Poetas del Mundo Azteca*, for biographies and compositions of thirteen poets of the Aztec world.
[2] *Códice Matritense de la Real Academia*, VIII, fol. 115 v.

and hopelessness these people are the true heirs of the ancient pre-Columbian wisdom.

In the native literatures of Mexico, both ancient and contemporary, remains the message of those who knew how to give meaning to life and the enigma of death, the ultimate reality and the universe. The texts, poems, and hymns which survive are witness to the truth spoken by the ancient wise men who had so often repeated that their flowers and songs, the art of the indigenous world, would exist forever. The famous Nezahualcóyotl said it in this way:

My flowers will not come to an end,
my songs will not come to an end,
I, the singer, raise them up;
they are scattered, they are bestowed. . . .[3]

[3] *Cantares Mexicanos*, fol. 16 v.

Bibliography

I. Primary Sources

Anales de Cuauhtitlán. In *Códice Chimalpopoca.* Photographic reproduction, study, and translation into Spanish by Primo F. Velázques. 2d. ed. Mexico City: National University of Mexico Press, 1975. Also in German; *Die Geschichte der Königreiche von Culhuacan und Mexico,* with an introduction and translation into German by Walter Lehmann. 2d. ed. Stuttgart, 1975.

Anales Históricos de la Nación Mexicana. Anales de Tlatelolco. Facsimile reproduction in *Corpus Codicum Americanorum Medii Aevi, 2.* Edited by Ernst Mengin. Copenhagen, 1945.

Anales de Quauhtinchan. Historia Tolteca-Chichimeca. Facsimile reproduction and translation by Luis Reyes and Odena Güemes. Mexico City: Instituto Nacional de Antropología e Historia, 1976.

Anales de los Xahil. From the French translation of Georges Reynaud, with an introduction by Francisco Monterde. Mexico City: Biblioteca del Estudiante Universitario, 1946.

The Annals of the Cakchiqueles and *Title of the Lords of Totonicapan.* Translated from the Cakchiquel Maya by Adrián Recinos and Delia Goetz. Norman: University of Oklahoma Press, 1967.

Barrera Vásquez, Alfredo. *El Libro de los Cantares de Dzitbalché.* Mexico City: Instituto Nacional de Antropología e Historia. 2d ed. Mérida, Yucatán, 1980.

―――. *El Libro de los Libros de Chilam Balam.* Mexico City: Fondo de Cultura Económica, 1948.

―――. *The Maya Chronicles.* Publication 585 of the Carnegie Institution of Washington. Washington, D.C., 1949.

Cantares Mexicanos. Facsimile reproduction of the manuscript in the National Library of Mexico. Edited by Antonio Peñafiel. Mexico City, 1904.

Caso, Alfonso. "Un códice en Otomí." *Proceedings of the XXIIIrd International Congress of Americanists*, pp. 130–35. New York, 1928.

―――. *Las estelas zapotecas.* Mexico City: Monografías del Museo Nacional, 1928.

―――. "Explicación del Reverso del Códice Vindobonensis." *Memorias del Colegio Nacional* (Mexico City), 5 (1952): 9–46.

―――. *Interpretación del Códice Bodley 2858.* Mexico City: Sociedad Mexicana de Antropología, 1960.

Chilam Balam, Books of. See Munro S. Edmonson, A. Barrera Vásquez, Ralph L. Roys.

Chimalpahin Cuauhtlehuanitzin, Domingo. *Diferentes Historias originales de los reynos de Culhuacan y México, y do otras provincias.* Translated and edited by Ernest Menguin. Hamburg, 1950. Facsimile reproduction in *Corpus Codicum Americanorum Medii Aevi, 3.* Edited by Ernst Mengin. Cophenhagen, 1949–52.

―――. *Das Memorial Breve acerca de la Fundación de la Ciudad de Culhuacan.* Edited by Walter Lehmann and Gerdt Kutscher. Stuttgart, 1958.

―――. *Die Relationen Chilampahin's zur Geschichte Mexiko's.* In *Abhandlungen aus dem Gebiet des Auslandskunde*, vols. 38–39. Edited by Günter Zimmermann. Hamburg, 1963, 1965.

―――. *Relaciones Originales de Chalco Amaquemecan.* Edited by Silvia Rendón. Mexico City: Fondo de Cultura Económica, 1965.

―――. *Sixième et Septième Relations (1358–1612).* Translated and published by Remi Simeón. Paris, 1889.

Codex Bodley 2858. See Alfonso Caso.

Codex Borbonicus. Mexican manuscript in the Library of the Palais Bourbon. Facsimile edition with commentary by Karl Anton Nowotny. Graz: Akademische Druck- und Verlagsanstalt, 1974.

Codex Borgia. Mexican manuscript in the Ethnographic Museum of the S. Congr. di Prop. Fide. Reproduced in facsimile with a commentary by Karl Anton Nowotny. Graz: Akademische Druck- und Verlagsanstalt, 1974.

Codex Dresden. In *Die Maya-handschrift der Koeniglichen Bibliotek zu Dresden*, ed. E. Förstemann, 2d ed. Leipzig, 1892.

Codex Fejérváry-Mayer. Pre-Columbian manuscript in the Free Public. Museum of Liverpool (M 12014). Facsimile edition with a commentary by C. A. Burland. Graz: Akademische Druck- und Verlagsanstalt, 1971.

Codex Madrid. Commentary by Ferdinand Anders. Graz: Akademische

Druck- und Verlagsanstalt, 1968.

Codex Mendoza. Edited and translated by James Cooper Clark. Graz: Akademische Druck- und Verlagsanstalt, 1938.

Codex Paris ("Peresianus"). Commentary by Ferdinand Anders. Graz: Akademische Druck- und Verlagsanstalt, 1938.

Codex Telleriano-Remensis. Mexican manuscript of the office of Ar. M. le Tellier, archbishop of Rheims, now in the Bibliothèque Nationale (MS Mex. 385). Paris: E. T. Hamy, 1899.

Codex Vaticanus A (Ríos). Vatican Mexican manuscript 3738, called the Ríos Codex. Reproduced in facsimile by the Duke of Loubat with the permission of the Vatican Library. Rome, 1900.

Códice Aubin (de 1576). Facsimile reproduction, edited and translated by Charles E. Dibble. Madrid, 1963.

Códice de Calkiní. Edited by Alfredo Barrera Vásquez. Campeche, Mexico: Biblioteca Campechana, 1957.

Códice Florentino. Preserved in the Laurentian Library, Florence. Facsimile reproduction. 3 vols. Mexico City: Archivo General de la Nación, 1979. In Bernardino de Sahagún, *Historia General de las Cosas de Nueva España*, translated and edited by Arthur J. O. Anderson and Charles E. Dibble. 12 vols. Santa Fe, N. Mex., and Salt Lake City: School of American Research and University of Utah, 1950–82.

Códice Matritense de la Real Academia de la Historia. Nahuatl texts of the Indian informants of Sahagún. Facsimile of vol. 8, edited by Francisco del Paso y Troncoso. Madrid: Hauser y Menet, 1907.

Códice Matritense del Real Palacio. Nahuatl texts of the Indian informants of Sahagún. Facsimile edition of vol. 6 (part 2) and vol. 7 by Francisco del Paso y Troncoso. Madrid: Hauser y Menet, 1906.

Códice Pérez. Edited by Hermilo Solís Alcalá. Mérida, 1949.

Códice Ramírez. The origin of the Indians of New Spain, according to their histories. Mexico City: Editorial Leyenda, 1944.

Cogolludo, Diego López de. *Historia de Yucatán.* 3 vols. Campeche, Mexico: Comisión de Historia, 1954.

Crónica de Chac-Xulub-Chen. Translated from the Maya by Héctor Pérez Martínez. In *Crónicas de la Conquista*, edited by Agustín Yáñez. Mexico City: Biblioteca del Estudiante Universitario, 1950.

Crónicas Indígenas de Guatemala. Edited by Adrián Recinos. Guatemala City: Editorial Universitaria, 1957.

Díaz del Castillo, Bernal. *Historia verdadera de la Conquista de la Nueva España*. 3 vols. Mexico City: Robredo, 1939.

———. *The Discovery and Conquest of Mexico, 1517–1521*. Translated and edited by A. P. Maudslay. New York: Grove Press, 1958.

Durán, Fray Diego. *Book of the Gods and Rites and the Ancient Calendar*. Translated and edited by Fernando Horcasitas and Doris Heyden. Foreword by Miguel León-Portilla. Norman: University of Oklahoma Press, 1971.

Edmonson, Munro S. *The Ancient Future of the Itza: The Book of Chilam Balam of Tizimin*. Austin: University of Texas Press, 1982.

———. *The Book of Counsel: The Popol Vuh of the Quiche Maya of Guatemala*. Middle American Research Institute Publication no. 35. New Orleans: Tulane University, 1971.

Estudios de Cultura Maya. Vols. 1–15. Seminario de Cultura Maya, Instituto de Historia. Mexico City: National University of Mexico, 1961–84.

Estudios de Cultura Náhuatl. Vols. 1–18. Seminario de Cultura Náhuatl, Instituto de Historia. Mexico City: National University of Mexico, 1959–85.

García Icazbalceta, Joaquín, ed. *Nueva Colección de Documentos para la Historia de México*. 5 vols. Mexico City, 1886–92.

Garibay K., Ángel María. *Épica Náhuatl*. Biblioteca del Estudiante Universitario, no. 51. Mexico City, 1945.

———. *Historia de la Literatura Náhuatl*. Mexico City: Editorial Porrúa, 1953–54.

———, trans. "Huehuetlatolli, Documento A." *Tlalocan* 1 (1943): 31–53, 81–107.

———. "Paralipómenos de Sahagún." *Tlalocan* 1 (1943–44): 307–313, 2 (1946): 167–74, 249–54.

———. *Poesía Náhuatl*. Vol. 1, *Romances de los Señores de la Nueva España*. Vols. 2–3, manuscript in the National Library of Mexico. Seminario de Cultura Náhuatl, Instituto de Historia. Mexico City: National University of Mexico, 1963, 1965, 1968.

———. "Relación Breve de las Fiestas de los Dioses (compiled by Bernardino de Sahagún)." *Tlalocan* 2 (1948): 289–320.

———. *Veinte Himnos Sacros de los Nahuas* (Informants of Sahagún, 2). Seminario de Cultura Náhuatl, Instituto de Historia. Mexico City: National University of Mexico, 1958.

———. *Vida Económica de Tenochtitlan* (Informants of Sahagún, 3). Seminario de Cultura Náhuatl, Instituto de Historia. Mexico City: National University of Mexico, 1960.

Gates, William. *The William Gates Collection*. New York: Press of J. J. Little and Ives, 1924.

Gómez de Orosco, Federico. *Crónicas de Michoacán*. Mexico City: Biblioteca del Estudiante Universitario, 1954.

Ixtlilxóchitl, Fernando de Alva. *Obras Completas*. 2 vols. Mexico City, 1891–92. New edition by Edmundo O'Gorman. 2 vols. Mexico City: UNAM, Instituto de Investigaciones Históricas, 1975.

Landa, Diego de. *Relación de las cosas de Yucatán*. Mexico City, 1938. A translation, edited and with notes by A. M. Tozzer, was published in the *Peabody Museum of American Archaeology and Ethnology Papers* (Harvard University), vol. 18 (1941). All footnote references are to the Héctor Pérez Martínez edition (Mexico City, 1938).

Lehmann, Walter. *Die Geschichte der Königreiche von Colhuacan und Mexico*. Vol. 1 in *Quellenwerke zur alten Geschichte Amerikas*. Contains texts of *Anales de Cuauhtitlán* and *Leyenda de los Soles* with German translation. Stuttgart, 1938; reprint, with an index, 1974.

————. *Sterbende Götter und Christliche Heilsbotschaft, Wechselreden Indianischer Vornehmer und Spanischer Glaubenapostel in Mexiko, 1524 [Colloquies and Christian Doctrine]*. Spanish and Mexican text with German translation. Stuttgart, 1949.

León-Portilla, Miguel. *Aztec Thought and Culture: A Study of the Ancient Náhuatl Mind*. Norman: University of Oklahoma Press, 1963.

————, ed. *The Broken Spears: Aztec Account of the Conquest of Mexico*. Boston: Beacon Press, 1961, 1966.

————. *Mesoamerican Spirituality*. New York: Paulist Press, 1980.

————. Ritos, Sacerdotes y Atavíos de los Dioses (Informants of Sahagún, 1). Seminario de Cultura Náhuatl, Instituto de Historia. Mexico City: National University of Mexico, 1958 and 1969.

Martínez Hernández, Juan. *Crónicas Mayas* (Maní, Tizimín, Chumayel). Mérida, Yucatán, 1926.

Memorial de Tecpan Atitlán. (*Anales de los Cakchiqueles*). By Francisco Hernández Arana Xajilá and Francisco Díaz Gebutá Quej. With notes and linguistic study by J. Antonio Villacorta C. Guatemala, 1934.

Mengin, Ernst, ed. *Historia Tolteca-Chichimeca. Corpus Codicum Americanorum Medii Aevi*, 1. Copenhagen: Sumptibus Einar Munksgaard, 1942.

———— and Konrad Preuss. *Die Mexikanische Bilderhandschrift Historia*

Tolteca-Chichimeca, Übersetz und erläutert von. . . . Parts 1 and 2. Berlin: Baesler Archives, 1937–38.

Motolinía, Toribio de Benavente. *Memoriales.* Paris, 1903.

———. *Historia de los Indios de la Nueva España.* Mexico City: Chávez Hayhoe, 1941.

Muñoz Camargo, Diego. *Historia de Tlaxcala.* Mexico City: Chavero, 1892.

Olmos, Andrés de. *Arte para aprender la lengua Mexicana.* Includes first part of *MSS en Náhuatl.* Paris, 1875; Guadalajara, Mexico, 1972.

———. *History of the Indians of New Spain.* Translated and edited by Elizabeth Andros Foster. Berkeley, Calif., 1950.

———. *MSS en Náhuatl (Huehuetlatolli).* The original is preserved in the Library of Congress, Washington, D.C.

Paso y Troncoso, Francisco del, ed. *Leyenda de los Soles.* Florence, 1903.

———. *Papeles de la Nueva España.* 9 vols. Madrid and Mexico, 1905–1948.

Peñafiel, Antonio. *Colección de Documentos para la Historia de México.* 6 vols. Mexico City, 1897–1903.

Pomar, Juan Bautista. *Relación de Texcoco.* Vol. 3 in *Nueva Colección de Documentos para la Historia de México,* edited by García Icazbalceta. Mexico City, 1891.

Popol Vuh. Translated by Dennis Tedlock with commentary based on the ancient knowledge of the modern Quiche Maya. New York: Simon and Schuster, 1985. See also Munro S. Edmonson.

Popol Vuh: Das heiliges Buch der Quiché Indianer von Guatemala. Quiché text and German translation. Edited by Leonhard Schultze-Jena. Stuttgart, 1943.

Popol Vuh: Las Historias Antiguas del Quiché. Translated from the original text with an introduction and notes by Adrián Recinos. Mexico City: Fondo de Cultura Económica, 1947.

Popol Vuh: The Sacred Book of the Ancient Quiché Maya. English translation by Delia Goetz and Sylvanus G. Morley from the Spanish by Adrián Recinos. Norman: University of Oklahoma Press, 1950.

Rabinal Achí, Teatro Indígena Prehispánico. Edited by Francisco Monterde. Mexico City: Biblioteca del Estudiante Universitario, 1955.

Ramesal, Fray Antonio de. *Historia de la Provincia de San Vicente de Chiapas y Guatemala.* 2 vols. Guatemala: Sociedad de Geografía e Historia, 1932.

Relación de Michoacán de las Ceremonias y Ritos y Población y Gobierno de los Indios de la Provincia de Mechoacán. Edited by José Tudela. Madrid: Aguilar, 1956.

Romances de los Señores de la Nueva España, Poesie Nahuatl I. Edited by Ángel María Garibay K. Mexico City: National University of Mexico, 1964.

Roys, Ralph L., ed. *The Book of Chilam Balam of Chumayel.* Publication 438 of the Carnegie Institution of Washington. Washington, D.C., 1933. New edition published by the University of Oklahoma Press, Norman, 1967.

―――. *The Book of Chilam Balam of Ixil.* Carnegie Institution of Washington Notes on Middle American Archaeology and Ethnology, no. 75. Cambridge, Mass., 1946.

―――. *Ritual of the Bacabs.* Norman: University of Oklahoma Press, 1965.

Sahagún, Bernardino de. *Historia General de las Cosas de Nueva España.*
Edited by Carlos María de Bustamante. 3 vols. Mexico City, 1829.
Edited by Robredo. 5 vols. Mexico City, 1938.
Edited by Miguel Acosta Saignes. 3 vols. Mexico City, 1946.
Edited by A. M. Garibay K. 4 vols. Mexico City: Porrúa, 1956.
All footnote references are to the A. M. Garibay K. edition.

Scholes, France V., and Ralph L. Roys. *The Maya Chontal Indians of Acalan-Tixchel.* Publication 560 of the Carnegie Institution of Washington. Washington, D.C., 1948. New edition published by the University of Olkahoma Press, Norman, 1968.

Schulze-Jena, Leonhard. *Alt-aztekische Gesänge, nach einer in der Bibl. Nacional von Mexiko aufbewahrten Handscrift, übersetz und erlaütert von. . . .* Vol. 6 in *Quellenwerke zur alten Geschichte Amerikas.* Stuttgart, 1957.

―――. *Gliederung des alt-aztekischen Volks in Familie Stand und Beruf, aus dem aztekischen Urtext Bernardino de Sahagún's.* Vol. 5 in *Quellenwerke zur alten Geschichte Amerikas.* Stuttgart, 1952.

―――. *Wahrsagerei, Himmelskunde und Kalender der alten Azteken, aus dem Aztekischen Urtext Bernardino de Sahagún's.* Vol. 4 in *Quellenwerke zur alten Geschichte Amerikas.* Stuttgart, 1950.

Seler, Eduard. *Einige Kapitel aus dem Geschichteswerk des P. Sahagún, aus dem Aztekischen übersetzt von Eduard Seler.* Edited by C. Seler-Sachs in collaboration with Walter Lehmann. Stuttgart, 1927.

―――. *Gesammelte Abhandlungen zur Amerikanischen Sprach- und Altertumskunde.* 5 vols. Berlin: Ascher und Co. and Behrend und Co., 1902–1923.

Sodi, Demetrio. *La literatura de los mayas.* Mexico City: Instituto Indigenista Interamericano, 1964.

Tezozómoc, F. Alvarado. *Crónica Mexicana.* Reprint. Mexico City: Editorial Leyenda, 1944.

————. *Crónica Mexicáyotl.* Paleography and Spanish version by Adrián León. Mexico City: Imprenta Universitaria, 1949.

Thompson, J. Eric S. *A Catalog of Maya Hieroglyphs.* Norman: University of Oklahoma Press, 1962.

————. *Maya Hieroglyphic Writing.* Norman: University of Oklahoma Press, 1960.

Torquemada, Fray Juan de. *Monarquía Indiana.* 3 vols. Reproduction of the 1723 Madrid edition. Introduction by Miguel León-Portilla. Mexico City: Editorial Porrúa, 1969.

Tozzer, Alfred M. "The Chilam Books and the Possibility of Their Translation." In *Proceedings of the XIXth International Congress of Americanists,* pp. 178–86. Washington, D.C., 1915.

————. *A Maya Grammar with Bibliography and Appraisement of the Works Noted. Papers of the Peabody Museum of American Archaeology and Ethnography* (Harvard University), 9 (1921). See also Diego de Landa, *Relación.* . . .

Ximénez, Francisco. *Historia de la Provincia de San Vicente de Chiapa y Guatemala de la Orden de Predicadores.* 3 vols. Guatemala City: Biblioteca Goathemala, 1929–31.

Zimmerman, Günter. *Die Hieroglyphen der Maya-Handschriften. Abhandlungen aus dem Gebiet der Auslandskunde* (Universität Hamburg), vol. 58, series B (1956).

2. SECONDARY SOURCES

Acosta, Joseph de, S.J. *Historia Natural y Moral de las Indias.* Mexico City: Fondo de Cultura Económica, 1940, 1962.

Anders, Ferdinand. *Das Pantheon der Maya.* Graz: Akademische Druck- und Verlagsanstalt, 1963.

Andrews, Richard. *Introduction to Classical Nahuatl.* Austin: University of Texas Press, 1975.

Barlow, Robert H. *The Extent of the Empire of the Culhua Mexica. Iberoamericana,* no. 28. Berkeley and Los Angeles: University of California Press, 1949.

Beaumont, Fray Pablo. *Crónica de Michoacán.* 2 vols. Mexico City, 1932.

Benson, Elizabeth P., ed. *Mesoamerican Writing Systems.* Washington, D.C.: Dumbarton Oaks Research Library and Collection, 1973.

Brinton, Daniel G. *The Maya Chronicles.* Library of Aboriginal American Literature, no. 1. Philadelphia, 1882.

————. *Rig-Veda Americanus*. Philadelphia, 1890.

Burgoa, Fray Francisco de. *Palestra historial de la provincia de predicadores de Guaxaca. Publicaciones del Archivo General de la Nación*, 24. Mexico City, 1934.

Carmack, Robert M. *Quichean Civilization: The Ethnographic and Archaeological Sources*. Berkeley: University of California Press, 1973.

Carrasco Pizana, Pedro. *Los Otomíes, cultura e historia prehispánica de los pueblos mesoamericanos de habla otomiana*. Mexico City: Instituto de Historia, National University of Mexico, 1950.

Caso, Alfonso. *The Aztecs: People of the Sun*. Norman: University of Oklahoma Press, 1958.

————. "Zapotec Writing and Calendar." In *Handbook of Middle American Studies*, ed. Robert Wauchope, 3: 931–47. Austin: University of Texas Press, 1965.

Clavijero, Francisco Javier. *Historia antigua de México*. 4 vols. Colección de Escritores Mexicanos. Mexico City: Porrúa, 1945.

Cline, Howard F., ed. "Guide to Ethnohistorical Sources." *Handbook of Middle American Indians*, ed. Robert Wauchope, 12–14. Austin: University of Texas Press, 1972–74.

Coe, Michael D. *The Maya Scribe and His World*. New York: Grolier Club, 1973.

Cornyn, John H. *The Song of Quetzalcoatl*. Yellow Springs, Ohio, 1930.

Corona Núñez, José. *Mitología tarasca*. Mexico City: Fondo de Cultura Económica, 1957.

Correa, Calvin Cannon, W. A. Hunter, and Barbara Bode, eds. *The Native Theatre in Middle America*. Middle American Research Institute Publication no. 27. New Orleans: Tulane University, 1961.

Dahlgreen de Jordan, Barbro. *La Mixteca, su cultura e historia prehispánicas*. Mexico City: National University of Mexico, 1954.

Dark, Philip. *Mixtec Ethnohistory: A Method of Analysis of the Codical Art*. Oxford University Press, 1958.

Díaz Vasconcelos, Luis Antonio. *Apuntes para la Historia de la Literatura Guatemalteca*. 2d ed. Guatemala City, 1950.

Dyck, Anne. *Mixteco Texts*. Edited by Benjamin Elson. Norman: Summer Institute of Linguistics, University of Oklahoma, 1959.

Edmonson, Munro S. *Quiche-English Dictionary*. Middle American Research Institute Publication no. 30. New Orleans: Tulane University, 1965.

————, ed. *Sixteenth Century Mexico: The Work of Sahagún*. A School of

American Research Book. Albuquerque: University of New Mexico Press, 1974.

Fernández, Justino. *Coatlicue, estética del arte indígena antiguo*. Prologue by Samuel Ramos. 2d ed. Mexico City: Centro de Estudios Filosóficos, 1959.

Galarza, Joaquín. *Estudios de escritura indígena tradicional azteca-náhuatl*. Mexico City: Archivo General de la Nación, 1979.

García, Fray Gregorio. *Origen de los indios de el Nuevo Mundo e Indias Occidentales*. Madrid, 1729.

Gay, José Antonio. *Historia de Oaxaca*. Mexico City, 1881.

Gillmor, Frances. *Flute of Smoking Mirror: A Portrait of Nezahualcóyotl, Poet-King of the Aztecs*. Albuquerque: University of New Mexico Press, 1949.

Gossen, Gary H. *Chamula in the World of the Sun: Time and Space in a Maya Oral Tradition*. Cambridge, Mass.: Harvard University Press, 1974.

Hernández, Francisco. *De Antiquitatibus Novae Hispaniae*. Facsimile edition of the *Códice Matritense de la Real Academia de la Historia*. Mexico City, 1926. Spanish translation by García Pimentel. Mexico City: Robredo, 1945.

Hunter, William A. "The Calderonian Auto Sacramental 'El Gran Teatro del Mundo,' An edition and translation of a Náhuatl version." In Calvin Cannon Correa, ed., *The Native Theatre in Middle America*. New Orleans: Middle American Research Institute, 1961.

Jiménez Moreno, Wigberto. "Fr. Bernardino de Sahagún y su obra." In Sahagún, *Historia general de las cosas de Nueva España* 1: *xiii–lxxxi*. Mexico City: Robredo, 1938.

Kelley, David Humiston. *Deciphering the Maya Script*. Austin: University of Texas Press, 1976.

Krickeberg, Walter von. *Altmexikanische Kulturen*. Berlin: Safari Verlag, 1956.

Kroeber, Alfred L. *Anthropology*. Rev. ed. New York: Harcourt, Brace, 1948.

La Rosa, Agustín de. *Estudio de la Filosofía y Riqueza de la Lengua Mexicana*. Guadalajara, 1889. Published in part in *Et Caetera*, no. 1 (March, 1950).

Lehmann, Walter. "Die Bedeutung der altamerikanischen Hochkulturen für allgemeine Geschichte der Menschheit." *Ibero-Americanisches Archiv*, April–July, 1943, pp. 65–71.

León, Nicolás. *Los Tarascos: Notas históricas, étnicas y antropológicas, comprendiendo desde los tiempos pre-colombinos hasta los actuales. . . .* First part. Mexico City: Imprenta del Museo Nacional de Mexico, 1904.

León-Portilla, Miguel. *Los Antiguos Mexicanos, a través de sus crónicas y cantares*. Mexico City: Fondo de Cultura Económica, 1961.

————. *Time and Reality in the Thought of the Maya.* Boston: Beacon Press, 1972.

————. *Trece Poetas del Mundo Azteca.* Mexico City: Institute of Historical Research, National University of Mexico, 1967.

McAfee, Byron, and Robert H. Barlow. *Diccionario de elementos fonéticos en escritura jeroglífica (Códice Mendocino).* Mexico City: Instituto de Historia, 1949.

Mediz Bolio, Antonio, ed. *El Libro del Chilam Balam de Chumayel.* San José, Costa Rica, 1930.

Morley, Sylvanus G. *La civilización maya.* Mexico City: Fondo de Cultura Económica, 1947.

Orozco, Gilberto, ed. *Tradiciones y Leyendas del Istmo de Tehuantepec.* Mexico City: Revista Musical Mexicana, 1946.

Orozco y Berra, Manuel. *Historia Antigua y de la Conquista de México.* 4 vols. 2d ed. Mexico City: Editorial Porrúa, 1959.

Parsons, Elsie C. "Zapotec and Spanish Tales of Mitla, Oaxaca." *Journal of American Folklore* 45 (1932): 318–62.

Pike, Kenneth L. "Una Leyenda Mixteca." *Investigaciones Lingüísticas* 4: 262–70. Mexico City, 1937.

Prem, Hanns J. "Aztec Hieroglyphic Writing System—Possibilities and Limits." *Verhandlungen des XXXVIII, Internationalen Amerikanistenkongresses, Stuttgart-München,* 2: 159–65. Munich, 1970.

————. "Calendrics and Writing: Observations on the Emergence of Civilization in Mesoamerica." In *Contributions of the University of California Archaeological Research Facility,* ed. Robert F. Heizer and John A. Graham, no. 11, pp. 112–32. Berkeley, Calif., 1971.

Radin, Paul. *An Historical Legend of the Zapotecs. Ibero-Americana* (Berkeley, Calif.), vol. 9 (1935).

Robertson, Donald. *Mexican Manuscript Painting of the Early Colonial Period.* New Haven: Yale University Press, 1959.

Sánchez de Aguilar, Pedro. *Informe contra Idolorum Cultores.* 3d ed. Mérida, Yucatán, 1937.

Schultze-Jena, Leonhard. *Leben, Glaube und Sprache der Quiché von Guatemala, Indiana I.* Jena, 1933.

Smith, Mary Elizabeth. *Picture Writing from Ancient Southern Mexico: Mixtec Place Signs and Maps.* Norman: University of Oklahoma Press, 1973.

Soustelle, Jacques. *La Famille Otomí-Pame du Mexique Central.* Paris, 1937.

———. *Le pensée cosmologique des anciens Mexicains*. Paris: Hermann et Cie., 1940.

Spence, Lewis. *The Civilization of Ancient Mexico*. Cambridge, England, 1912.

———. *The Gods of Mexico*. London, 1923.

——— *The Magic and Mysteries of Mexico*. London, n.d.

Spinden, Herbert J. *Ancient Civilization of Mexico and Central America*. New York, 1943.

Tedlock, Barbara. "Sound Texture and Metaphor in Quiché Maya Ritual Language." *Current Anthropology* 23 (1982): 269–72.

———. *Time and the Highland Maya*. Albuquerque: University of New Mexico Press, 1982.

Tedlock, Dennis. "Las formas del verso Quiché." In *Nuevas Perspectivas sobre el Popol Vuh*, ed. Robert M. Carmack and Francisco Morales Santos, pp. 123–32. Guatemala: Piedra Santa, 1983.

———. *The Spoken Word and the Work of Interpretation*. Philadelphia: University of Pennsylvania Press, 1983.

Thompson, J. Eric S. *Commentary on the Dresden Codex*. Philadelphia: American Philosophical Society, 1972.

———. *The Rise and Fall of Maya Civilization*. 2d ed., 1966. Norman: University of Oklahoma Press, 1954.

Toscano, Salvador. *Arte Pre-colombino de México y de la América Central*. 4th ed. Mexico City: Instituto de Investigaciones Estéticas, 1984.

Vaillant, George C. *The Aztecs of Mexico: Origin, Rise and Fall of the Aztec Nation*. New York: Doubleday, 1941.

Veytia, Mariano. *Historia Antigua de México*. 2 vols. Mexico City: Editorial Leyenda, 1944.

Walcot, E. Emmart. *The Badianus Manuscript*. Baltimore: Johns Hopkins Press, 1940. New facsimile edition. Mexico City, 1964.

Weitlaner, Roberto. "Canciones Otomies." *Journal de la Société des Americanistes de Paris* 27 (1935): 303–324.

Yoneda, Keiko. *Los mapas de Cuauhtinchan y la historia cartográfica prehispánica*. Mexico City: Archivo General de la Nación, 1981.

Index

Acalan: 167

Aesthetics: applied to pre-Columbian creations, 81–83

Agriculture: texts related to, 33, 39–40, 72, 96, 100–102

Ahuianime (public women): 98, 112–15, 140

Ahuítzotl (an Aztec king or *tlatoani*): 112, 114, 145, 160

Alva Ixtlilxóchitl, Fernando de: 153

Alvarado, Pedro de: 143–45, 161–62, 169–72

Alvarado Tezozómoc, F.: *see* Tezozómoc

Annals and native chronicles: 116–31; in the Maya languages, 120–24, 143–45, 165–72; in Náhuatl, 116–20, 124–30, 153–64; in Otomí, 24

Aquiauhtzin (a Náhuatl poet): 82

Archaeological monuments: 43, 61, 96, 116

Archaeology: applied to check early native sources, 116

Architecture: 48, 55

Art: native concepts of, 67, 81–83, 138, 174; artistic creations, 138

Artists: 40–41, 48, 55, 174–75

Authorship of the pre-Columbian compositions: 58, 66, 78, 174

Axayácatl (an Aztec king): 160, 162

Ayocuan Cuetzpaltzin (a Náhuatl poet): 78, 81–83, 174

Azcapotzalco: 119

Aztecs: 31, 33, 42–48, 55, 58, 77, 87–88, 98–99, 116, 117, 119, 126, 130–31, 133–34, 141, 150–64, 169; their literary capacity, 42; their cultural evolution, 126–27, 130–31

Bacabs: 50

Barrera Vásquez, Alfredo: 120

Battles, literary descriptions of: 42–48, 49–50, 87–88, 96, 122–23, 143–44, 161–62, 163, 170–71

Benavente, Fray Toribio de (Motolinía): 149

Beyond, native concept of the: 33–34, 61–62, 81, 83–86, 89, 99, 102

Birds: 33, 41, 42, 50, 61, 62, 86, 89, 90, 92, 94, 98, 108–109, 154, 165

Black and red inks (symbol of wisdom): 32, 42, 58, 109, 124, 125, 130, 139

Bourbourg, Charles E. Brasseur de: 103

Brinton, Daniel G.: 60

Buffoons: 106–109

Cakchiquel Mayas: 121, 122–23, 144–45, 150, 169–72

Calendar in Mesoamerica: 97, 116, 118, 125; among the Mayas, 69, 116, 124, 165; among the Nahuas, 99, 149, 163

Calkiní (Campeche): 20

Calmécac (native centers of learning): 97, 98, 100; *see also* education

Cantares mexicanos (the manuscript): 94, 112

Causeways: 159, 162, 163

189

Pre-Columbian Literatures of Mexico was set on the Linotype in eleven-point Granjon with two points of leading between the lines. One of the most readable of type faces, Granjon is a modern type based on classic letter forms.

The drawings at the chapter openings were made from illustrations taken from ancient Mexican texts, all of which are discussed in this book.

The paper selected for *Pre-Columbian Literatures of Mexico* bears the watermark of the University of Oklahoma Press and is designed to have an effective life of over three hundred years.

UNIVERSITY OF OKLAHOMA PRESS : NORMAN